1 MONTH OF
FREE
READING

at

www.ForgottenBooks.com

By purchasing this book you are eligible for one month membership to ForgottenBooks.com, giving you unlimited access to our entire collection of over 1,000,000 titles via our web site and mobile apps.

To claim your free month visit:

www.forgottenbooks.com/free249474

ISBN 978-0-266-23723-5
PIBN 10249474

A CATALOGUE

OF THE

PORTSMOUTH COLLECTION OF
BOOKS AND PAPERS

WRITTEN BY OR BELONGING TO

SIR ISAAC NEWTON

C. J. CLAY AND SONS,

CAMBRIDGE UNIVERSITY PRESS WAREHOUSE,

AVE MARIA LANE.

Cambridge: DEIGHTON, BELL, AND CO.

Leipzig: F. A. BROCKHAUS.

A CATALOGUE

OF THE

PORTSMOUTH COLLECTION

OF BOOKS AND PAPERS

WRITTEN BY OR BELONGING TO

SIR ISAAC NEWTON

THE SCIENTIFIC PORTION OF WHICH
HAS BEEN PRESENTED BY THE EARL OF PORTSMOUTH
TO THE UNIVERSITY OF CAMBRIDGE

*DRAWN UP BY THE SYNDICATE APPOINTED
THE 6th NOVEMBER 1872*

CAMBRIDGE
AT THE UNIVERSITY PRESS
1888

CAMBRIDGE:
PRINTED BY C. J. CLAY, M.A. AND SONS,
AT THE UNIVERSITY PRESS.

CONTENTS.

CATALOGUE.

SECTION I.

SECTION II.

* These have been returned to Lord Portsmouth.

*SECTION III.

PAGE

*SECTION IV.

*SECTION V.

SECTION VI.

SECTION VII.

SECTION IX.

*SECTION X.

*SECTION XI.

*SECTION XII.

*SECTION XIII.

*SECTION XIV.

*SECTION XV.

* These have been returned to Lord Portsmouth.

PREFACE.

IT has been long known that Sir Isaac Newton left, at his death, a large mass of papers, consisting partly of copies of his works written out or corrected for the press, partly of notes relating to the various subjects in which he was interested, and of an extensive correspondence with English and Foreign mathematicians. These came immediately on his death into the possession of Mr Conduitt, who married Catharine Barton, Newton's favourite and accomplished niece. By the marriage of their only child to the first Lord Lymington, they passed into the hands of the first Lord Lymington, and we find them in October 1751 in the hands of Mr Saunderson of Sheer Lane, for Lord Lymington[1]. Since that time they have remained in the possession of the Portsmouth family.

Several years ago the present Earl of Portsmouth expressed a wish to present to the University all that portion of the papers and correspondence which related to science, as he felt that these would find a more appropriate home in the Library of Newton's own University than in that of a private individual. Lord Portsmouth entrusted the whole collection of papers to the University, and the present syndicate was appointed to examine, classify, and divide them. This has proved a lengthy and laborious business, as many of the papers were found to be in great confusion—mathematical notes being often inserted in the middle of theological treatises, and even numbered leaves of MSS. having got out of order. Moreover a large portion of the collection has been grievously damaged by fire and damp. The

[1] See Stukeley's *Memoirs* (Surt. Soc., 1887) iii. p. 15.

correspondence, however, is in a very fair condition throughout, and had been arranged in an orderly manner.

On receiving a preliminary report on the contents of the collection, Lord Portsmouth expressed a wish that the papers relating to Theology, Chronology, History, and Alchemy, should be returned to him at Hurstbourne, where they would be carefully preserved. On account of his connection with the Newton family, Lord Portsmouth also naturally wished to have returned to him all the papers relating to private, personal, and family matters. These, however, are comparatively few, and not of much interest, with the exception of a short note from Newton's mother, written to him when a boy at College.

Although till the present time the papers have never been thoroughly examined, they have been looked at and partially used by various persons since Newton's death. When that occurred (in 1727) Dr Pellett was appointed by the executors to examine them and to select such as he deemed fit for publication. A rough catalogue of the papers is appended to a bond given by Mr Conduitt to the administrators of Newton's estate, in which he binds himself to account for any profit he may make by their publication. This list, with some remarks of Dr Pellett, will be found in Hutton's Mathematical Dictionary. All which Dr Pellett deemed fit to be printed were *An Abstract of the Chronology* in 12 half-sheets folio, and *The Chronology of Ancient Kingdoms Amended* in 92 half-sheets folio; and these were printed in 1728 under the care of Mr Conduitt.

The whole collection was inspected by Dr Horsley, who edited in 1779 the well-known edition of Newton's works in five quarto volumes. He left a few unimportant remarks on some of the papers, but he made no use of them in his edition.

It was again placed in the hands of Sir David Brewster, for his second and elaborate life of Newton in 1855; he made some use of the scattered mathematical notes and papers, and printed a considerable portion of the correspondence.

and Alchemy, Chronology, History, and Theology. Many of the Mathematical papers contain Newton's preparations for the *Principia,* and notes which spring out of questions that were started by his correspondents. It must be recollected that Newton practically gave up his mathematical studies after 1696, even the superintendence of the second edition of the *Principia* being given to Cotes, and thus that after this date there is little of value in these subjects; and as most of what is contained in them, especially all that relates to the revision of the *Principia,* has been published, there is little to be found beyond what has already appeared.

The case is different, however, with respect to the papers referring to three subjects, viz. 1st, the Lunar Theory, 2nd, the Theory of Atmospheric Refraction, and 3rd, the Determination of the Form of the Solid of Least Resistance.

It is expressly stated by Newton himself that the Lunar Theory as given in his *Principia* is a mere specimen or fragment of the subject, intended to show how some of the more prominent lunar inequalities could be traced to the disturbing action of the Sun, and how their amounts could be calculated approximately by theory.

The only part which is developed with any fulness of detail is that relating to the inequality called the variation, and also that which treats of the motion of the node and the change of inclination of the orbit to the ecliptic.

In a short scholium given in the first edition of the *Principia,* Newton mentions that by similar computations he has found the motion of the moon's apogee, and he states some of the numerical results which he has obtained, but he does not give the calculations themselves, as he considers them too complicated and not sufficiently accurate.

In the second edition this short scholium is replaced by a long one, in which Newton states many of the principal results of the Lunar Theory, partly as found from theory alone and partly as deduced by combining his theory with observation; but he confines himself to results alone, and does not give the method by which these results have been obtained. Unfortunately also, the statement given in the first edition, as to the result which he had found by theory for the motion of the moon's apogee, is omitted in the new scholium.

It is interesting to find among the papers on the Lunar Theory a good many containing Newton's calculations relating to the inequalities which are described in the above scholium. These papers are unfortunately very imperfect, and they have greatly suffered from fire and damp, but there is enough remaining to give a general idea of Newton's mode of proceeding. The most interesting of these papers relate to the motion of the moon's apogee. Two lemmas are first established which give the motion of the apogee in an elliptic orbit of very small eccentricity due to given small disturbing forces acting, (1) in the direction of the radius vector, and (2) in the direction perpendicular to it.

These lemmas are carefully written out, as if in preparation for the press, and they were probably at first intended to form part of the *Principia*.

Next follows the application of the lemmas to the particular case of the Moon, in which the supposition that the disturbances are represented by changes in the elements of a purely elliptic orbit of small eccentricity would lead to practical inconvenience, and consequently Newton is led to modify that supposition. In the *Principia* he shows that if the moon's orbit be supposed to have no independent eccentricity, its form will be approximately an oval with the earth in the centre, the smaller axis being in the line of syzygies and the larger in that of quadratures, the ratio of these axes being nearly that of 69 to 70. Now when the proper eccentricity of the orbit is taken into account, supposing that eccentricity to be small, Newton assumes that the form of the orbit in which the moon really moves will be related to the form of the oval orbit before mentioned, nearly as an elliptic orbit of small eccentricity with the earth in its focus is related to a circular orbit about the earth in the centre. He then attempts to deduce the horary

moon's apogee when in that position is to the mean hourly
motion of the moon as

$$1 + \tfrac{11}{2}C : 238\tfrac{3}{10}.$$

The investigation on this point is not entirely satisfactory,
and from the alterations made in the MS. Newton evidently
felt doubts about the correctness of the coefficient $\tfrac{11}{2}$ which
occurs in this formula.

From this, however, he deduces quite correctly that the
mean annual motion of the apogee resulting would amount
to 38° 51′ 51″, whereas the annual motion given in the Astronomical Tables is 40° 41$\tfrac{1}{2}$′.

The result stated in the scholium to the 1st Edition appears
to have been found by a more complete and probably a much
more complicated investigation than that contained in the
extant MSS.

The papers also contain a long list of propositions in the
Lunar Theory which were evidently intended to be inserted in
a second edition, upon which Newton appears to have been
engaged in 1694. This list, together with the two lemmas on
the motion of the apogee mentioned above, will be found in
the Appendix.

Halley inserted in the *Philosophical Transactions* of 1721 a
Table of Refractions by Newton, without giving any idea of
the method of its formation.

Kramp, in his *Analyse des Réfractions*, published in 1799,
investigates by a new and powerful analytical method the law
of atmospheric refraction for rays in the neighbourhood of the
horizon.

On comparing his theoretical results with Newton's Table,
he finds a remarkably close agreement, which is enough to show
that the Table was also the result of theory, and therefore that
Newton must have had some method of his own of solving the
difficult problem of horizontal refraction.

Nothing was known of this method, however, until the publication of the correspondence between Newton and Flamsteed
by Mr Baily in 1835. In a letter to Flamsteed, dated December 20th, 1694[1], Newton tries to explain the foundation of

[1] Baily's *Flamsteed* p. 145.

his theory of refraction by giving a theorem from which it is
clear that Newton then understood how to form the differential
equation to the path of a ray of light through our atmosphere.
It is true that, for the sake of greater simplicity in this com-
munication to Flamsteed, Newton restricts the enunciation of
his theorem to the particular case where the density decreases
uniformly as the height increases, but it is obvious from the
form of the enunciation of Newton's theorem that the method
is general, provided that the differential of the density which is
appropriate to any given law of diminution be employed in
finding the corresponding differential of the refraction.   In an
interesting article in the *Journal des Savants* for 1836, M. Biot
directs particular attention to this subject, and tries to repro-
duce the method which Newton may be supposed to have
employed in order to calculate his table of refractions.   M. Biot
closes his article in the following terms :—

"Il est donc prouvé, par ce qui précède, que Newton a formé
l'équation différentielle exacte de la réfraction pour les atmosphères
de composition uniforme; qu'il l'a appliquée exactement au cas où
les densités des couches sont proportionelles aux pressions, ce qui
rend leur température constante; et qu'enfin, pour ce cas, il a obtenu
les vraies valeurs des réfractions à toute distance du zénith, sans
avoir eu besoin d'employer les intégrations analytiques qu'il a dû
très-vraisemblablement ignorer.   Il est donc le créateur de cette
théorie importante de l'astronomie physique, qui serait probablement
aujourd'hui plus perfectionée, si l'on avait connu plus tôt ses premiers
efforts."

portions of the path, and from these the actual refractions in passing over these portions are derived by making the total horizontal refraction equal to the amount given by observation. It should be remarked that the above calculation requires an approximate knowledge of the path of the ray, whereas this path is at first unknown, and cannot be accurately determined without a knowledge of the refraction itself. Newton solves the difficulty by an indirect method, making repeated approximations to the form of the path, and thus at length succeeding in satisfying all the required conditions.

The papers show that the well-known approximate formula for refraction commonly known as Bradley's was really due to Newton. This formula is only applicable when the object is not very near to the horizon, but the method of calculation employed by Newton is equally valid whatever be the apparent zenith distance.

It is well known that in the *Principia* Newton determines the form of the solid of least resistance, thus affording the first example of a class of problems which we now solve by means of the Calculus of Variations. He there gives what is equivalent to the differential equation to the curve by the revolution of which the above-named solid is generated, without explaining the method by which he has obtained it. Now among the Newton papers we have found the draft of a letter to a correspondent at Oxford, no doubt Professor David Gregory, in which Newton gives a clear explanation of his method, which is very simple and ingenious. The draft has no date, but from internal evidence it was probably written about 1694. A small part of the letter has perished but it is very easy to restore the missing portion. The letter will be found in the Appendix at the end of this preface. It may be remarked that a similar method is immediately applicable to the problem of finding the line of quickest descent.

A great many of the Newton papers relate to the dispute with Leibnitz about the discovery of Fluxions or the Differential Calculus. They show that Newton's feelings were greatly excited on this subject, and that he considered that

Leibnitz had shown towards him in reference to it great unfairness and want of candour. Newton always maintained that Leibnitz was the aggressor in this dispute, and that he had, by his language in the Leipsic Acts, covertly accused him of plagiarism, whereas he might have known from the correspondence that formerly took place between them, that Newton's method was in his possession long before he himself became acquainted with the Differential Calculus.

On the other hand Leibnitz, without avowing himself the author of the article in the Leipsic Acts, denied that it really bore the meaning attributed to it by Newton, and maintained that Newton had either been deceived by a false friend into imagining that he had been accused of plagiarism, or else that he was not sorry to find a pretext for attributing to himself the invention of the new Calculus, contrary to the avowal he had made in the Scholium in the 1st Edition of the *Principia*.

From a paper by Leibnitz, which has been published by Dr Gerhardt, it appears that the article in the Leipsic Acts, of which Newton complained, was really written by Leibnitz, and it also seems probable that the ambiguity of its language was not unintentional. We cannot wonder, then, that Newton, firmly believing that Leibnitz had charged him with plagiarism, should have experienced a strong feeling of resentment, and should have been induced to retort the charge upon his accuser[1]. It was not unnatural that this embittered feeling should still survive even after the death of Leibnitz.

It is clear from these Portsmouth papers that Newton believed that Leibnitz, during his second visit to England in October 1676, had obtained access to his MS. entitled *De Analysi per Equationes numero terminorum infinitas*, which was in the hands of Collins, and that he had thus been materially assisted in discovering the Differential Calculus. This tract of Newton's is printed in full in the *Commercium*

been seen by Leibnitz. There can now be no doubt, however, that Newton was right in thinking that Leibnitz had been shown this MS., since a copy of part of it, in Leibnitz's hand, has been found among the papers of Leibnitz preserved in the Royal Library at Hanover[1]. It is, of course, possible that at the time when this copy was taken Leibnitz was already acquainted in some degree with the Differential Calculus, but it is difficult to acquit him of a want of candour in never avowing in the course of the long controversy respecting the discovery of Fluxions, that he had not only seen this tract of Newton's, but had actually taken a copy of part of it. He must have seen, also, at the same time, that the MS. was an old one, and although it does not contain the pointed letters which Newton sometimes but by no means invariably employed to denote Fluxions, Leibnitz could hardly fail to see, if he was acquainted with the Differential Calculus, that the principle of Newton's method was the same as that of his own. It is repeatedly stated by Newton that what he claims is the first invention of the method, and that he does not dispute about the particular signs and symbols in which the method may be expressed. Again, he often states that although, in the sense which he employs, the method can have but one *inventor*, yet the method may be improved, and the improvements belong to those who make them.

In some of these papers relating to the dispute with Leibnitz, Newton gives us some interesting information respecting the times when several of his discoveries were made. Thus in a passage, which has been quoted by Brewster[2], he states that he wrote the *Principia* in seventeen or eighteen months, beginning in the end of December 1684, and sending it to the Royal Society in May 1686, excepting that about ten or twelve of the propositions were composed before, viz. the 1st and 11th in December 1679, the 6th, 7th, 8th, 9th, 10th, 12th, 13th and 17th, Lib. I, and the 1st, 2nd, 3rd and 4th, Lib. II, in June and July 1684. The following extract will give an idea of Newton's prodigious mental activity at an earlier period of his life.

[1] See Gerhardt, *Mathem. Schriften Leibnitzens*, I. p. 7.
[2] Brewster's *Life*, Vol. I. p. 471.

"In the beginning of the year 1665 I found the method of approximating Series and the Rule for reducing any dignity of any Binomial into such a series. The same year in May I found the method of tangents of Gregory and Slusius, and in November had the direct method of Fluxions, and the next year in January had the Theory of Colours, and in May following I had entrance into the inverse method of Fluxions. And the same year I began to think of gravity extending to the orb of the Moon, and having found out how to estimate the force with which [a] globe revolving within a sphere presses the surface of the sphere, from Kepler's Rule of the periodical times of the Planets being in a sesquialterate proportion of their distances from the centers of their orbs I deduced that the forces which keep the Planets in their Orbs must [be] reciprocally as the squares of their distances from the centers about which they revolve: and thereby compared the force requisite to keep the Moon in her orb with the force of gravity at the surface of the earth, and found them answer pretty nearly. All this was in the two plague years of 1665 and 1666[1], for in those days I was in the prime of my age for invention, and minded Mathematicks and Philosophy more than at any time since. What Mr Hugens has published since about centrifugal forces I suppose he had before me. At length in the winter between the years 1676 and 1677[2] I found the Proposition that by a centrifugal force reciprocally as the square of the distance a Planet must revolve in an Ellipsis about the center of the force placed in the lower umbilicus of the Ellipsis and with a radius drawn to that center describe areas proportional to the times. And in the winter between the years 1683 and 1684[3] this Proposition with the Demonstration was entered in the Register book of the R. Society. And this is the first instance upon record of any Proposition in the higher Geometry found out by the method in dispute. In the year 1689 Mr Leibnitz, endeavouring to rival me, published a Demonstration of the same Proposition upon another supposition, but his Demonstration proved erroneous for want of skill in the method."

The above extract has been given here on account of its intrinsic interest, although in writing it so many years after the events to which it relates, Newton appears to have made one or two mistakes of date, and probably for this reason has drawn his pen through the entire passage.

Newton's manuscripts on Alchemy are of very little interest in themselves. He seems to have made transcripts from a variety of authors, and, if we may judge by the number of praxes of their contents which he began and left unfinished, he seems to have striven in vain to trace a connected system in the processes described. He has left, however, notes of a number of his own chemical experiments made at various dates between 1678 and 1696. Some of these are quantitative. Those of most interest relate to alloys. He mentions several easily fusible alloys of bismuth, tin and lead, and gives as the most fusible that which contains 5 parts of lead + 7 of tin + 12 of bismuth. He says that an alloy consisting of 2 parts of lead + 3 of tin + 4 of bismuth will melt in the sun in summer. The alloy which goes by his name is not in the proportions of either of these two; but, as he states that tinglas (bismuth) is more fusible than tin, he could not have used pure metal.

The note-book which contains the longest record of his chemical experiments contains also the account of a few optical and other physical experiments and the paper on the decussation of the optic nerve published by Harris and from him by Brewster. Harris, according to Brewster, published from a copy in the Macclesfield Collection; but the copy seems to have been identical with that in this book, except that a paragraph at the end is omitted. Brewster overlooked the paper in this book, though he has quoted from other parts of the book.

The Historical and Theological MSS. cannot be considered of any great value. A great portion of Newton's later years must have been spent in writing and rewriting his ideas on certain points of Theology and Chronology. Much is written out, as if prepared for the press, much apparently from the mere love of writing. His power of writing a beautiful hand was evidently a snare to him. And his fastidiousness as to the expression of what he wrote comes out very curiously in these

papers; thus there are six drafts of the scheme for founding the
Royal Society, seven drafts of his remarks on the chronology
published under his name at Paris (which made him very angry),
many of the Observations on the Prophecies, several of the
scheme of mathematical learning proposed for Christ's Hospital,
&c.

The four elaborately bound volumes, containing 'the Chronology of Ancient Kingdoms Amended,' the Chronicle to the
Conquest of Persia by Alexander, Observations on the Prophecies, and the treatise "De Mundi Systemate," are very remarkable specimens of their author's care in writing out his works,
and of his beautiful handwriting (§ vii. 2). They are all contained in Horsley's collection.

It is believed that in the present catalogue nothing has
been omitted, and that thus a very fair idea may be obtained of
what occupied Newton's time throughout his life. The papers
date from his earliest time, giving his accounts when first he
began college life as a sizar of Trinity College, and his mathematical notes while still an undergraduate: and they continue
till his death. All the papers or books which have been returned to Lord Portsmouth are marked with an asterisk * in
the catalogue. Of the more important letters, which have not
been retained by the University, copies have been taken by
the permission of Lord Portsmouth, and these are retained with
the portion of the MSS. presented by him to the University.
In addition to this a copy of Brewster's Life of Newton has
been placed with the collection, in which the letters there given
have been carefully collated with their originals; so that practically the student of Newton's works has all the scientific
correspondence at his command.

H. R. LUARD.
G. G. STOKES.
J. C. ADAMS.

APPENDIX TO THE PREFACE.

IT may be interesting to give a few extracts from the Newton papers on some of the subjects which have been referred to in the above Preface. These relate to

    I.   The form of the Solid of Least Resistance. *Principia*, Lib. II. Prop. 35, Schol.

    II.   A List of Propositions in the Lunar Theory intended to be inserted in a second edition of the *Principia.*

    III.   The motion of the Apogee in an elliptic orbit of very small eccentricity, caused by given disturbing forces.

I. ON THE FORM OF THE SOLID OF LEAST RESISTANCE.

LIB. II., PROP. XXXV. SCHOL., p. 326, 1st Ed.

Draft of a Letter in Newton's hand, no doubt to Professor David Gregory, and probably written in 1694.

SIR,

    I now thank you heartily both for the very kind visit you made me here and for the errata you gave me notice of in my book and also for your care of Mr Paget's business. The Lem. 1 in the third book I could not recover as tis there stated, but I have don't another way with a Demonstration, and altered very much the Proposition which follows upon it concerning the precession of the Equinox. The whole is too long to set down. The figure which feels the least resistance in the Schol. of Prop. xxxv. Lib. II. is demonstrable by these steps.

1. If upon BM be erected infinitely narrow parallelograms $BGhb$ and $MNom$ and their distance Mb and altitudes MN, BG be given, and the semi sum of their bases $\dfrac{Mm + Bb}{2}$ be also given and called s and their semi difference $\dfrac{Mm - Bb}{2}$ be called x: and if the lines BG, bh, MN, mo, butt upon the curve $nNgG$ in the points n, N, g, and G, and the infinitely little lines on and hg be equal to one another and called c, and the figure $mnNgGB$ be turned about its axis BM to generate a solid, and this solid move uniformly in water from M to B according to the direction of its axis BM:

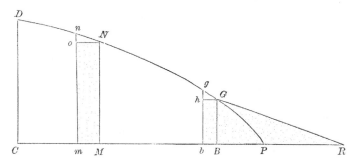

the summ of the resistances of the two surfaces generated by the infinitely little lines Gg, Nn shall be least when gG^{qq} is to nN^{qq} as $BG \times Bb$ to $MN \times Mm$.

For the resistances of the surfaces generated by the revolution of Gg and Nn are as $\dfrac{BG}{Gg^{\text{quad}}}$ and $\dfrac{MN}{Nn^{\text{ quad}}}$, that is, if Gg^{quad} and Nn^{quad} be called p and q, as $\dfrac{BG}{p}$ and $\dfrac{MN}{q}$ and their summ $\dfrac{BG}{p} + \dfrac{MN}{q}$ is least when the fluxion thereof $-\dfrac{BG \times \dot{p}}{pp} - \dfrac{MN \times \dot{q}}{qq}$ is nothing, or $-\dfrac{BG \times \dot{p}}{pp} = +\dfrac{MN \times \dot{q}}{qq}$.

Now $p = Gg^{\text{quad}} = Bb^{\text{quad}} + gh^{\text{quad}} = ss - 2sx + xx + cc$ and therefore $\dot{p} = -2s\dot{x} + 2x\dot{x}$, and by the same argument $\dot{q} = 2s\dot{x} + 2x\dot{x}$ and

2. If the curve line $DnNgG$ be such that the surface of the solid generated by its revolution feels the least resistance of any solid with the same top and bottom BG and CD, then the resistance of the two narrow annular surfaces generated by the revolution of the [infinitely little lines nN] and Gg is less then if the intermediate solid $bgNM$ be removed [along CB without altering Mb, until bg comes [to BG], supposing as before that on is equal to hg,] and by consequence it is the least that can be, and therefore gG^{qq} is to nN^{qq} as $BG \times Bb$ [is to $MN \times Mm$].

*[Also if] gh be equal to hG so that the angle [gGh is 45^{degr}] then will $4Bb^{qq}$ be [to nN^{qq} as $BG \times Bb$ is to] $MN \times Mm$, and by consequence $4BG^{qq}$ is to GR^{qq} as BG^{q} is to $MN \times BR$ or $4BG^{q} \times BR$ is to GR^{cub} [as GR to MN].

Whence the proposition to be demonstrated easily follows.

But its to be noted that in the booke pag 327 lin. 7 instead of *Quod si figura DNFB* it should be written *Quod si figura DNFGB*, and that $DNFG$ is an uniform curve meeting with the right line GB in G in an angle of $135^{degr.}$

I have not yet made any experiments about the resistance of the air and water nor am resolved to see Oxford this year. But perhaps the next year I may. I had answered your letter sooner but that I wanted time to examin this Theorem and the Lem. 1 in the 3^d Book. I do not see how to derive the resistance of the air from the ascent of water. The reasoning which must be about it seems too complicate to come under an exact calculus, and what allowance must be made for the retardation of the water by the contact of the pipe or hole at its going out of the vessel is hard to know.

II.   List of Propositions apparently intended to be inserted in a 2nd Edition of the Principia.

In Theoria Lunae tractentur hae Propositiones.

8 Prop. XXV.   Prob. v.   Page 434, Princip.

Orbem Lunae ad aequilibrium reducere.

* If the altitude of the frustum of the cone spoken of in the preceding paragraph be infinitely small, the semi-angle of the cone becomes equal to 45°. Hence when the total resistance is a minimum, the curve meets the extreme ordinate GB at an angle of 45°.

5 Prop. XXVI.

Aream orbis totius Lunaris in plano immobili descriptam mensi synodico proportionalem esse.

6 Prop. XXVII.

Invenire distantiam mediam Lunae a Terra.

7 Prop. XXVIII.

Invenire motum medium Lunae.

1 Prop. XXIX.

In mediocri distantia Terrae a Sole invenire vires solis tam ad perturbandos motus Lunae quam ad mare movendum.

2 Prop.

Invenire vires Lunae ad mare movendum.

3 Prop. XXX.

Invenire incrementum horarium areae quam Luna in orbe non excentrico revolvens radio ad terram ducto in plano immobili describit.

4 Prop. XXXI.

Ex motu horario Lunae invenire distantiam ejus a terra.

10 Prop.

Invenire formam orbis Lunaris non excentrici.

11 Prop.

Invenire variationem Lunae in orbe non excentrico.

9 Prop.

Invenire aequationem parallacticam.

12 Prop.

Invenire formam orbis Lunaris excentrici.

13 Prop.

Invenire incrementum horarium areae quam Luna in orbe excentrico revolvens radio ad terram ducto in plano immobili describit.

PROP.

Invenire aequationem parallacticam in orbe excentrico.

PROP.

Invenire parallaxim solis.

PROP.

Invenire motum horarium Apogaei Lunaris in Quadraturis consistentis.

PROP.

Invenire motum horarium Apogaei Lunaris in conjunctione et oppositione consistentis.

PROP.

Ex motu medio Apogaei invenire ejus motum verum.

De Sole.

PROP.

Invenire locum solis.

Ex Solis motu medio et prostaphaeresi dabitur locus centri gravitatis Terrae et Lunae deinde ex hoc loco et parallaxi menstrua (quae in quadraturis Lunae est 20″ vel 30″ circiter) dabitur locus terrae cum loco opposito solis.

PROP.

Invenire motum Apheliorum.

PROP.

Invenire motum nodorum.

Nodus orbium Jovis et Saturni movetur in plano immobili quod transit per nodum illum & secat angulum orbium in ratione corporum in distantias ductorum inverse, id est in ratione equalitatis circiter, existente angulo quem hoc planum continet cum angulo orbis Jovis minore quam angulo altero quem continet cum orbe Saturni. Serventur forte inclinationes orbium omnium ad hoc planum, & quaerantur motus intersectionum quas orbes cum ipso faciunt et habebuntur motus planorum orbium respectu fixarum.

PROP.

Invenire perturbationes Orbis Saturni ab ejus gravitate in Jovem oriundas.

PROP.

Invenire perturbationes Orbis Jovis ab ejus gravitate in Saturnum oriundas.

PROB.

In systemate Planetarum invenire planum immobile.

A centro solis per orbes Planetarum ducatur linea recta sic ut si Planetae singuli in minimas suas ab hac linea distantias ducantur, summa contentorum ad unam lineae partem aequetur summa contentorum ad alteram; et haec linea jacebit in plano immobili quam proxime.

Vel sic accuratius:

Per solem et orbes Planetarum et commune centrum gravitatis eorum omnium ducatur linea recta sic ut si sol et semisses Planetarum in minimis orbium ab hac linea distantiis ad utramque solis partem siti augeantur vel minuantur in ratione distantiarum verarum a centro solis ad distantias mediocres ab eodem centro, deinde ducantur in distantias suas ab hac linea: summa productorum ab una rectae parte et ab una etiam parte communis centri gravitatis, conjuncta cum summa productorum ex altera utriusque parte aequetur summae productorum reliquorum: jacebit haec recta in plano immobili, et hujusmodi rectae duae planum illud determinabunt.

III.   ON THE MOTION OF THE APOGEE IN AN ELLIPTIC ORBIT OF VERY SMALL ECCENTRICITY.

From a somewhat mutilated MS. which seems to have been prepared for the press.

LEMMA.

Si Luna P in orbe elliptico QPR axem QR, umbilicos S, F habente, revolvatur circa Terram S et interea vi aliqua V a pondere

P, et ratione lineae SE quae centro Terrae et perpendiculo PE interjacet ad umbilicorum distantiam SF.

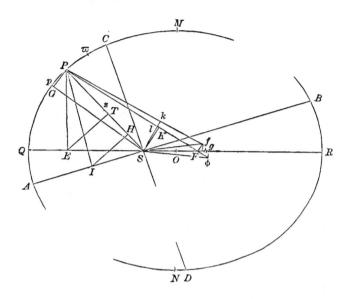

Cas. 1. Fingamus vires P & V non esse continuas sed singulis temporis particulis aequalibus et quam minimis semel agere, agat autem vis utraque in P sintque πP particulae ellipseos quas Luna praecedente temporis particula descripsit. Pp particula ejusdem Ellipseos [quam Luna] per impulsum vis solius P absque impulsu vis V posteriore temporis particula describere deberet et PG particula orbis novi quem Luna per impulsum vis utriusque V & P in loco P factum eadem posteriore temporis particula describit. Et erit angulus pPG ad angulum quem lineola pP cum lineola proximè ante appulsum Lunae ad locum P descripta et producta contineat, id est ad angulum PSG seu motum angularem Lunae ut vis V qua angulus prior genitus est ad vim ponderis P qua angulus posterior genitus est. Agatur Pf ea lege ut angulus fPG complementum sit anguli SPG ad duos rectos et Pf transibit per umbilicum superiorem Ellipseos novae, et quoniam angulus FPp, (ex natura Ellipseos) complementum sit anguli SPp ad duos rectos, angulus FPf duplo major erit angulo pPG, adeoque eam habebit rationem ad angulum PSG quam habet vis $2V$ ad vim P. Sit f umbilicus iste superior, et in PF ac Pf demittantur perpendicula SK et Sk, quorum Sk secet PF in l. Et per ea quae in Prop.   Lib. 1 ostensa sunt, erit PF ad $SP + PF$ ut ellipseos

latus rectum quod nominabimus L ad $2SP + 2PK$, et divisim PF [erit ad] SP ut L ad $2SP+2PK-L$, seu PF aequalis $\dfrac{L \times SP}{2SP + 2PK - L}$, et [eod]em argumento Pf aequalis $\dfrac{L \times SP}{2SP + 2Pk - L}$. Nam latus rectum quod sit (per Prop.   Lib. 1. Princip.) in duplicata ratione areæ quam Luna radio ad terram ducto singulis temporis particulis describit, et quantitas areæ illius per impulsum vis V nil mutetur, idem manet in Ellipsi utraque. Cum autem $2SP$ et L ob infinitè parvam distantiam SF aequentur, deleatur $2SP-L$ et erit FP aequalis $\dfrac{SP^{\prime}}{PK}$ et Pf aequalis $\dfrac{SP^{\prime}}{Pk}$ quarum differentia est $\dfrac{SP^{\prime} \times lK}{PK^{q}}$ seu lK. Est autem lK ad lk ut SK ad Pk, ideoque (ob infinite parvam SF) est lK infinite minor quam lk seu Ff, et propterea Ff perpendicularis est ad PK. Quare si jungatur Ef, anguli FEf & FPf, in segmento circuli per puncta P, E, F, f transeuntis consistentes, aequales erunt inter se. Ideoque cum angulus FSf sit ad angulum FEf ut FE vel SE ad FS seu $2OS$, et angulus FPf supra fuerit ad angulum PSG ut vis $2V$ ad vim P: erit ex aequo angulus FSf ad angulum PSG, id est motus Apogaei ad motum medium Lunae ut $2V \times SE$ ad $P \times SF$ seu $V \times SE$ ad $P \times OS$. Concipe jam numerum impulsuum augeri et intervalla diminui in infinitum ut actiones virium V et P reddantur continuae et constabit Propositio. Q. E. D.

Corol.   Valet Propositio quam proximè ubi excentricitas finitae est magnitudinis, si modo parva sit.

Lemma.

Si Luna P in orbe Elliptico QPR axem QR et umbilicos S, F habente revolvatur circa Terram, et interea vi aliqua W a pondere suo diversa secundum lineam distantiae SP perpendicularem impellatur; sit autem excentricitas OS infinite parva: erit motus Aphelii[1] ab

CAS. 1. Distinguatur enim tempus in particulas aequales et quam minimas, et agat vis W non continuò sed singulis temporis particulis semel. Sit autem T velocitas Lunae [in] P ante impulsum vis W ibi factum et t incrementum [velo]citatis ex impulsu et L latus rectum Orbis Lunaris ante [impulsum]. Et quoniam area quam Luna radio ad Terram [ducto singulis tem]poris particulis aequalibus describit, sit ante impulsum ad eandem aream post impulsum ut T ad $T + t$, et latus rectum (per Prop. xiv. Lib. i. Princip.) sit in duplicata ratione areæ, erit (per Lem. Lib. ii. Princip.) $\dfrac{T + 2t}{T} L$ seu $L + \dfrac{2t}{T} L$ latus rectum post impulsum. Est autem (ut in Lemmate superiore) $\dfrac{SP \times L}{2SP + 2PK - L}$ longitudo PF qua Luna distabat ab umbilico superiore ante impulsum; et propterea cum situs lineae PF, si modo excentricitas SF infinitè parva sit, ex impulsu illo nil· mutetur, ideoque PK maneat eadem quae prius et solum L mutetur, si producatur PF ad ϕ ut sit ϕ umbilicus superior post impulsum;

erit $P\phi$ aequalis $\dfrac{SP \times \dfrac{T + 2t}{T} L}{2SP + 2PK - L - \dfrac{2t}{T} L}$. De hac longitudine subdu-

catur longitudo ipsius PF superius inventa, nempe $\dfrac{SP \times L}{2SP + 2PK - L}$, et interea in utraque pro $2SP + 2PK$ scribatur $2L$ & manebit differentia $F\phi$ aequalis $\dfrac{4t}{T - 2t} SP$ seu $\dfrac{4t}{T} SP$. Unde longitudo perpendiculi ϕg quod in diametrum QR ab umbilico ϕ demittitur, crit $\dfrac{4t}{T} PE$. Jam vero in Lemmate superiore, velocitas quam vis V impulsu unico generare potest, est ad velocitatem Lunae ut lineola pG quam Luna vi impulsus illius dato tempore describere posset ad lineolam Pp quam Luna velocitate sua data T eodem tempore describat, id est ut Ff ad PF.[1] Ideoque si velocitas prior nominetur S crit Ff aequalis $\dfrac{2S \times PF}{T}$ ob angulum FPf anguli GPp duplum, et perpendiculum fh quod ab umbilico f in ellipseos axem QR demittitur aequale $\dfrac{2S}{T} EF$. Proinde cum angulus ϕSF sit ad angulum FSf ut ϕg ad fh, et angulus FSf ad angulum PSp ut $V \times SE$ ad $P \times OS$,

---

[1] This should be pG ad Pp.

crit angulus ϕSF ad angulum PSp, hoc est motus Apogaei a vi W genitus ad motum medium Lunae ut $\frac{4t}{T} PE$ ad $\frac{2S}{T} EF$ et $V \times SE$ ad $P \times OS$ conjunctim, id est (ob aequales EF ad SE et proportionales t & S, W & V) ut $2W \times PE$ ad $P \times OS$. Q.E.D.

COROL. Obtinet etiam Propositio quam proxime ubi [quam minima sit] excentricitas etiamsi non sit infinitè parva.

SECTION I.

MATHEMATICS.

I. EARLY PAPERS BY NEWTON. (Holograph.)

1. Extracts by Newton
   From Hooke's Micrographia,
   From the History of the Royal Society,
   From the Philosophical Transactions.
   Notes of some Mines in Derbyshire and Cardiganshire.

2. Scraps and Extracts made by Newton, including two little notes on tangents and musical semi-tones.

3. A tract in English written in 1666, entitled "To resolve problems by Motion."
Also short tracts entitled
   De Solutione Problematum per Motum.
   De Gravitate Conicarum.
   Problems of Curves.

4. Calculation of the Area of the Hyperbola.

5. On the Laws of Motion.
   On the Laws of Reflection.
   On Motion in a Cycloid.

6. Problems in Geometrical Optics.

———————————————

II. Elementary Mathematics. (Holograph.)

1. Observations on the Algebra of Kinckhuysen.

2. The first Ten Propositions of the 2nd book of Euclid, succinctly enunciated and demonstrated.

3. Theorem on the Area of a Triangle.

4. Trigonometria succinctè proposita et nova methodo demonstrata a St Joanne Hareo Arm.

5. A few MS. leaves, containing Compendium Trigonometriae. It includes Spherical Trigonometry. Intended for learners.

6. Table of sines to every half degree.

III. Fluxions.

1. Transcript of a Tract on Fluxions said to have been written by Newton in November, 1666.

2. Tract relating to the History of Fluxions, transcribed from one which was probably written by Jones.

3. Part of Newton's method of Fluxions and Infinite Series, with a fragment of the same treatise. (Holograph.)

4. Part of a Tract on Fluxions.

5. Some Propositions in Fluxions. [" I think this fragment very proper to be published." Horsley, Oct. 22, 1777.]

6. Analysis per quantitates fluentes et eorum momenta.

7. Method of Fluxions and Infinite Series.

8. On the solution of Fluxional Equations.

9. Fluxions applied to Curves.

10. Propositions in the Method of Fluxions (dotted letters employed).

11. Propositions in Fluxions (dotted letters employed).

12. An early paper on deducing the subnormal in a curve from a given rational relation between x and y, and the converse operation.

13. Fragments on Fluxions.

14. Method of Curves and Infinite Series, and application to the Geometry of Curves. Complete all but the 1st leaf.

3. On the curves of the third order, produced by the projections of the Parabola Neiliana.

4. Fragments concerning lines of the third order, and some mistakes of Descartes ["not worth publishing." S. Horsley, Oct. 23, 1777].

V. On the Quadrature of Curves. (Holograph.)

1. A copy which appears to be pretty complete.
2. A fragment on the same subject.
3. Scattered papers on the same subject, in great confusion
4. Another fragment on the same.
5. Note on Quadrature of Curves, intended as a Supplement to Section 10 of Book I. of the Principia.
6. Fragment on the Quadrature of Curves whose equations consist of but three terms.

VI. Papers relating to Geometry. (Holograph.)

1. De Problematum resolutione Synthetica.
2. Geometria. Liber 1. A fragment.
3. Geometry, a fragment on Porisms.
4. Analysis Geometrica.
   Regula Datorum.
5. Newton's Regula Fratrum.
6. Fragment relating to Curves.
7. Geometria Curvilinea and Fluxions.
8. Scraps containing Propositions in Geometry; viz.:
   (a) To describe a Conic Section through five given points; and
   (b) To describe a Conic Section passing through two points and touching three given straight lines.
9. Tract on the construction of Equations, unfinished.
10. On the Properties of Curves.
11. Part of a Treatise on Geometry (in Latin).
12. De Compositione Locorum Solidorum.
13. Solutio Problematis Veterum de Loco Solido.
14. Fragments relating to the writings of the Ancients in general, but especially to the Porisms of Euclid, and the Loci of

Apollonius ["very curious and fit to be published." S. Horsley, Oct. 26, 1777].

15.   Remarks on the nature and objects of Arithmetic, Geometry, and Mechanics.

16.   A fragment, relating to the Comparison of Curved Superficies.

VII.   MISCELLANEOUS MATHEMATICAL SUBJECTS. (Holograph, exc. 7.)

1.   Problemata Numeralia.

2.   Arithmetica Universalis.   A chapter on the limits of the roots of equations (see p. 184 of Leyden Ed. of Univ. Arith. 1732).

3.   De serierum proprietatibus.

4.   On Quadrature by Ordinates.

5.   Regula differentiarum &c.

6.   Bernouilli's problem on drawing lines cutting a series of curves according to any given law.   Phil. Trans. 1716.

7.   Errata in Dr Barrow's Conicks and in his Archimedes, with a letter to Newton about the latter Errata.

8.   Scraps of calculations.

VIII.   PAPERS CONNECTED WITH THE PRINCIPIA. (Mostly Holograph.)

A.   *General.*

1.   Propositions on Elliptic Motion.

2.   A fragment in which Fluxions are employed in finding the Centripetal force in an Orbit.

3.   Propositions afterwards included in the Principia, but differently numbered.

4.   A small fragment (early) of the Principia.

5.   De Motu Corporum.

6.   Propositiones De Motu Corporum.

The references do not agree with the Principia.

7.   Propositiones de Motu.

Several copies differing somewhat from each other, of which one is printed in Rigaud's " Historical Essay " Appendix, No 1.

8.   Corrections to copy of Propositions on Motion forming probably an early draft of part of the Principia.

9.   Proposed Corrections probably for 1st Edition of the Principia.

11.   Revision of the Principia.   Notes relating to Calculation of orbits of Comets.

12.   Additions and Corrections to 1st Edition of the Principia.

13.   Additions and Corrections to the 2nd Edition of the Principia.

14.   Observations and Calculations about Comets.

15.   Draft of part of the Preface to the 1st Edition of the Principia.   Not quite as printed, in part fuller.

16.   Preface and Preparations for 3rd Edition of the Principia.

17.   Very rough fragments relating to the Principia.

18.   Miscellaneous Calculations.

19.   Corrections to 1st Edition of the Principia (terribly damaged by fire).

20.   Dr Halley's account of the Principia given to K. James II.

IX.   Papers connected with the Principia.

B.   *Lunar Theory.*

1.   Papers on the Lunar Theory found in interleaved copy of 1st Edition of Principia (damaged by fire).

2.   Propositions prepared to be used in the Lunar Theory (greatly damaged by fire).

3.   Fragments on the Lunar Theory (greatly damaged by fire).

4.   Propositions in the Lunar Theory, found on loose sheets placed at the end of the interleaved copy of the 1st Edition of the Principia.

These were probably intended to be employed in a 2nd Edition, but the design was not carried out.

5.   Notes on the law of change of the Moon's variation according to the change of the Sun's distance; and on the mutual action of Jupiter and Saturn.

6.   Unarranged fragments connected with points of the Lunar Theory.

7.   On change of the variation in an excentric orbit, and on the motion of the Moon's Apogee.

8.   A list of Propositions in the Lunar Theory, prepared for a 2nd Edition of the Principia, but not used.

9. Propositions relating to the Lunar Theory, including a Scholium, differing from that inserted in the 2nd Edition.

10. On the Theory of the Moon.

(Various statements of the principal points of this Theory.)

11. Propositions 'De motu nodorum Lunæ,' prepared for the 3rd Edition of the Principia.

12. Motion of the Moon's Apogee. This consists of two Lemmas, prepared for press; two Propositions, in duplicate; and an imperfect copy of one of these propositions, with a rough draft of an investigation of the horary variation of the Inclination.

The Propositions are not numbered, and therefore they were perhaps intended to be worked up for the 1st Edition.

13. Calculations for forming Lunar Tables.

14. Various Lunar Tables.

15. Comparisons of calculated places of the Moon with Observations.

X. PAPERS CONNECTED WITH THE PRINCIPIA.

C. *Mathematical Problems.*

1. To find the True Anomaly from the Mean.

2. Fragment on the Solid of least resistance.

3. Atmospheric Refraction, with detailed calculation of the Refraction at the altitudes 0°, 3°, 12° and 30°.

4. Altitudes by the Barometer.

XI. PAPERS RELATING TO THE DISPUTE RESPECTING THE INVENTION OF FLUXIONS.

1. Apographum Schediasmatis a Newtono olim scripti, 13 Nov. 1665.

2. Printed Title-page of the 1st Edition of the Commercium

6. Enarratio plenior Scholii præcedentis.

7. Mens Scholii præcedentis.

8. An account of the Commercium Epistolicum (several varying copies).

9. Papers relating to the origin of the Dispute.

10. Collations for the History of the Infinitesimal Analysis.

11. Fragment of "An account of the Differential Method from the year 1677 inclusively."

12. History of the Method of Fluxions. (Several copies with varying Titles.)

13. "Historia Methodi Infinitesimalis" (several varying copies), with Corrigenda to the English copy of the "Recensio" published in Phil. Trans. Jan., Feb., 1714–5.

14. Annotationes in Commercium Epistolicum.

15. Appendix containing Newton's proofs of his priority to Leibnitz, &c. (A fragment.)

16. Newton's Statement of the case in dispute between Leibnitz and himself.

17. Draft (holograph) of Newton's Letter to the Editor of Memoirs of Literature, May, 1712 (never published). (See Brewster, ii. 283.)

18. Copy in Newton's hand of Leibnitz's letter to Hans Sloan, 29th Dec., 1711.

19. References to the original letters contained, or intended to be contained, in the Commercium Epistolicum.

20. Latin translation (copy) of the Recensio given in Phil. Trans. No. 342, differing from that given in the Second Edition of the Commercium Epistolicum.

21. 'Ad Lectorem,' prefixed to the 2nd Edition of the Commercium Epistolicum. (Several drafts.)

22. Latin letter (copy) of John Keill to Hans Sloan. May, 1711.

23. Keill's letter (copy) to John Bernouilli, translated into French after July, 1716, with some notes on it in Newton's hand.

24. Extract from a letter of Leibnitz complaining of an attack on his "bonne foi."

25. Bernouilli's problem in the Acta Eruditorum for Oct. 1698.

26. Historical Annotations on the Elogium of Leibnitz.

27.   Several drafts of letters of Newton to Des Maizeaux after the death of Leibnitz.   (Holograph.)

28.   Remarks on Leibnitz's first Letter to the Abbé Conti.

29.   Proposed addition to the "Remarks" on Leibnitz's second Letter to the Abbé Conti—after Leibnitz's death.   (Des Maizeaux, Vol. 2, pp. 82–106.)

30.   Drafts of a letter to a friend of Leibnitz (probably Chamberlayne), defending Keill.   Also copy of English translation of Leibnitz's letter to Chamberlayne (in Newton's hand).

31.   Copy by Newton of Leibnitz's letter of 9th Ap. 1716, to De Monmort, and draft of Newton's Observations upon it given in Raphson's Hist. of Fluxions, App. p. 111.

32.   Newton's observations on the Synopsis given in the Leipzic Acts of Jones's "Analysis per quantitatum Series," &c. (Lond. 1711).

33.   Animadversions on Monmort's letter to N. Bernouilli, dated 20th Aug. 1713, and printed in the 2nd Edition of his Analysis upon the play of Hazard.

34.   John Bernouilli's letter of 7th June, 1713, with Newton's Observations upon it.

35.   Extract from Bernouilli's Notice of July, 1713 (the Charta Volans), and "Remarques sur la dispute entre Mons. Leibnitz et Mons. Newton," &c., with Newton's Observations upon them.

36.   Contents of Des Maizeaux's Recueil, &c.   Copies of letters which are published in Des Maizeaux's Recueil.

37.   Several drafts of an intended Preface to the Commercium Epistolicum.

38.   Letter of Newton to the Abbé Conti in reply to the Postscript of Leibnitz to the same. This letter refers to the 1st Postscript given in Des Maizeaux.

39.   Draft of part of the "Account of the Commercium Epistolicum," &c., inserted in the Phil. Trans.

40.   Errata in Raphson's History of Fluxions.

41.   Unarranged fragments relating to the dispute with Leibnitz.

42.   Drafts of Letters of Newton to Varignon and others, relating to Bernouilli's Letter of 7 June, 1713, which had been

XII. Astronomy.

1. Astronomical communications from Flamsteed, including longitudes and latitudes of stars for 1686, and of 21 stars compared with the comet of 1680.

2. Lunar distances in 1677 and in 1685, by Flamsteed, with copies of these two papers, one by Newton.

3. Equations of Moon's Apogee. Table by Newton for Flamsteed.
Elements of the Comets of 1472, 1580, 1585, 1652, 1661, 1665, 1672, 1677, and 1686, as calculated by Halley.

4. Eclipse Tables for a period of 18 years, by Halley.

5. Observations of Eclipses, sent to Newton from various quarters, with a diagram of the annular eclipse of 1686 by E. de Louville (Paris).

6. Transits of Satellites of Jupiter and of their shadows across the disc of the planet, observed by Pound at Wanstead.

7. Table of Declinations of every 5th degree of the Zodiac.

XIII. Hydrostatics, Optics, Sound, and Heat.

1. A treatise, with a table, on the Division of a Monochord. Not in Newton's hand, but apparently of his composition. Followed by an extract in his hand "out of Mr Sympson's Division Violist."

2. Scrap relating to the velocity of sound; also on the back a note on the proportionality of mass to weight.

3. Manuscript copy of Newton's Optical writings, and of controversies about them.

4. Latin draft of the Opticks, Book I., Part I. (1 sheet).

5. Answer to objections made to Newton's Optical Theories.
Also a scrap with memoranda about the Newtonian telescope.

6. Scrap. Memorandum of observations on the colours of thick plates.

7. Fragments on Light and Heat.

8. Proposed addition to Newton's Opticks.
On the Refraction observed in Iceland Spar, and Note "to the Reader" relating to it.

9.   Fragments on Opticks.

10.   Optical experiments.

11.   Figure and description of a sheep's eye. Printed by Brewster i. 420.

12.   Speculations as to the constitution of matter and the nature of the action of heat.

XIV.   MISCELLANEOUS COPIES OF LETTERS AND PAPERS.

1.   Copies of Letters from Leibnitz, Slusius, &c. to Oldenburgh.

2.   Copies of various Mathematical papers by Tschirnhausen, Leibnitz, Slusius, &c.

3.   "Sur la Cubature du coin Spherique" par M. de Lagny.

4.   Fragments on Mathematical subjects by Cassini, Craig, and Morland.

XV.   PAPERS ON FINDING THE LONGITUDE AT SEA.

1.   Various proposals for finding the Longitude at Sea.

2.   Several drafts of a Report by Newton to the Lords of the Admiralty on the different projects for determining the Longitude at Sea.

3.   Draft of a letter by Newton on the same subject.

4.   Two shorter drafts of the same letter.

SECTION II.

*I. FIVE PARCELS CONTAINING TRANSCRIPTS FROM VARIOUS ALCHEMICAL AUTHORS IN NEWTON'S HANDWRITING, WITH NOTES AND ABSTRACTS.

(1)

1. Notes out of Philalethes.

2. On Ripley's Vision; 'Sir G. Ripley his letter to K. Ed. IV. unfolded.'

3. 3 tracts. De metallorum metamorphosi, Brevis manductio ad rubinum cælestem, Fons Chemicæ Philosophiæ.

4. Extracts from Raymond Lully.

5.   ,,   ,,   an author unnamed.

6.   ,,   ,,   various authors.

7. "Artephius, his secret book."

8. Basil Valentine; on the minerals of Hungary, Carinthia &c., and the conditions of their formation, and on the transmutation of metals and the separation of the three principles, and of vitriol.

Jodochus a Rehe; Processes for preparing the Philosopher's stone from MSS. in possession of Dr Twysden. Copies of 4 letters from Faber to Dr Twysden, 1673—4, recounting success of experiments in preparing spirits of mercury.

Notes on Faber's work.

9. Hermes. Tabula smaragdina et commentarium.

10. The same in English.

11. "The Epitome of the treasure of health written by Edvardus generosus Anglicus innominatus, who lived A. D. 1562."

12. Hadrian Mynsicht. Aureum seculum redivivum. Testamentum de philosophorum lapide. Both in hexameters.

13. Ex Turba philosophorum.

14. Preparatio Mercurii, ex MSS. Philosophi Americani.

15. Liber Mercuriorum Corporum.   On the back an explanation of the symbols in it.

16. 47 Alchemical recipes, the work of an old Priest, viz. B.

17. Ex Rosario magno.

18. Emblemata Michaelis Maieri, comitis Germani.

19. Of chemical authors and their writings.

20. Collectiones ex novo lumine chemico.

21. Ex codicillo R. Lullii (Colon. 1563).

22. Notes mythological and alchemical.

23. Account of furnaces, &c.

24. Extracts from Flamel and several other authors.

25. A page of references to a work not named.

26. Loca difficilia in novo lumine Chymico explicata.

27. Extracts: clavis aureæ portæ, medulla Alchemiæ, de Lapide vegetabili, Pupilla Alchemiæ, &c.

28. Basil Valentini Currus triumphalis antimonii.

29. Alphabetical explanation of common chemical words.

30. Miscellaneous references.

31. Abstract of a treatise on Nature's obvious laws and processes in vegetation.

32. 'Out of Schroder's Pharmacopœia.'

(2)

1. The book of N. Flamel, in English.

2. The metamorphoses of the planets, with two folios of notes which are in the nature of memoranda of points adverted to in the treatise.

3. Maier's tracts:

Symbola aureæ mensæ duodecim nationum (an account of chemical writers in 12 books).

4.   Notanda chymica.   Out of Maier (1 f.).

5.   Regulæ...de lapide philosophico authore anon. and Maier's figures prefixed to Valentine's keys (1 f.).

6.   Ex Epistola Edm. Dickenson ad Theodorum Mundanum (2 f.).

7.   Tabula Smaragdina and other extracts.   Hieroglyphica Planetarum (1 f.).

8.   Extracts apparently from Van Helmont.   On the 3rd page, last line but two, occurs "Terra juxta parallelos rotunda est, juxta meridianos ovalis.   Hallucinatur."

9.   Notes chiefly from Philalethes on Ripley.

10.   On Ripley's gates (2 f.).

11.   Ripley expounded (2 f.).

12.   Notes on Ripley (an abstract).

13.   Thesaurus thesaurorum, in English (1 f.).

14.   A key to Snyders.

15.   Sententiæ notabiles expositæ (1 f.).

16.   Sententiæ luciferæ et conclusiones notabiles (4 f.).   A note relating to mint affairs on top of first page.

17.   Practica Mariæ Prophetissæ in artem Alchemicam (1 f.).

18.   De igne sophorum et materia quam calefacit (1 f.) extr. from various authors.

19.   Notanda chemica from various authors (1 f.).

20.   De secreto solutionis (1 f.) from various authors.

21.   The three fires.   The work with sol vulgar.   The several works (1 f.).

22.   "Clavis."

23.   Extracts from various authors, chiefly alchemical, but some notes also about the occurrence of minerals (1 f.).

24.   Verses at the end of B. Valentine's mystery of the microcosm.

25.   The standing of the glass for the time of Putrefaction.   The hunting of the Green Lyon, in verse, with some notes by Newton.

26.   "Pearce the black monck upon the Elixir" (verse).

27.   "Out of Bloomfield's Blossoms, and a short work that beareth the name of Sir George Ripley."

28.   Extracts from Norton's ordinal, Chaucer's tale of the Chanon's yeoman, the work of Richard Carpenter, Dastin's dream.

29.   Several questions concerning the Philosopher's stone, no author named (1 f.).

30. Observations of the matter in the glass, Authore Anonymo ; also a recipe for an elixir (1 f.).

31. Sendivogius explained (4 f.).

32. The same in Latin, an abstract (2 f.).

33. Epistola ad veros Hermetis discipulos. S. Didier.

34. The seven chapters of Hermes, with part of an unfinished letter on the back.

35. Latin letter communicated by Frederick duke of Holstein, 1656, giving an account of the death of a Jewish magician, of his oratory, instruments, perpetual fire in a crystal, &c. with no writer's name (1 f.).

(3)

1. Jodochus a Rehe.   Procédé universelle.

2. Artephius, de arte occulta lib. secretus.

3. Abstract of Flamel's account of his hieroglyphics with a sketch of the figures.

4. Novum lumen Chymicum Sendivogii (abstract).

5. Extracts from Joh. Spagnetus.   Enchiridion Physicæ, arcanum Hermeticæ Philosophiæ opus.

6. Extracts from Norton's Ordinal, Dastin's dream, Black monk, the hunting of the Green Lyon, Ripley, &c.

7. Ex Augurelli Chrysopœia, and the Marrow of Alchemy.

8. Extracts from Ripley and others.   Tabula Smaragdina, and De metallorum metamorphosi (a leaf missing at the beginning).

9. Observanda.   Instructio de Arbore Solari.   Arca Arcani. Epistola Grassæi.   Occultæ naturæ mysterium.   Appendix ad aurum potabile.   Lucerna salis philosophorum.   Auriga chemicus.   Rosarium magnum.

10. Snyders' Commentatio de Pharmaco Catholico.

11. References to B. Valentine's works, his process, 12 keys, and Extracts from his Testament.

12. Miscellaneous Notes and quotations.

16. Table of contents of some work on Alchemy.

17. Notes and memoranda (2 f.).

18. Abstract of some work, with commencement of a letter to Mr Proctor an attorney relating to a bond of Mr Tongue to Newton on the back.

19. Annotationes, being extracts from several works.

20. Account of S. Didier's keys, and what various other authors have written on the same subject. This seems to be an attempt to co-ordinate the accounts of processes described mystically by the several authors (5 f.).

21. Chemical nomenclature of the Egyptians, and a praxis of alchemy extracted from various authors, with a duplicate folio partly cancelled.

22. De mineralibus. Extracts from Geber and others.
References and extracts (one on the back of a letter).

23. Diagram of lapis philosophicus cum rotis elementaribus.

24. Memoranda about chemicals.

25. Notes of some process. On the back of memoranda of sums owing from Mr George Gates, Mr Day, and Richard Rawlins.

26. Receipt for some compound of sulphur, mercury, antimony and silver, apparently with a view to multiplication of the silver.

27. Alchemical receipts.

28. Receipts for medicines, ink, etc.

29. Table of contents of some work.

30. Part of a treatise, containing
Lapidis compositio, out of L. Ventura,
Elementorum conversio, from the same,
Regimen ignis, from the same and Is. Hollandus,
Materia, out of Philalethes and others,
Decoctio, Regimen Mercurii, Saturni, Jovis, Lunæ, Veneris, Martis, et Solis, out of various authors, and a rough copy of part of the Decoctio.

31. Another treatise in the form of extracts from various authors, some parts repeated, altered, and fragmentary; part Latin, part English, but no original matter.

32. Tables of contents to a similar treatise.

33. Another treatise, apparently earlier, edges partly burnt.

34. Table of contents, with a chapter de virga mercurii.

35. A collection of nine papers in a cover (originally ten), consisting of notes and extracts, the 10th paper, of ancient hieroglyphics, missing.

36. Three odd papers on the Regimen.

(4)

1. A common-place book, in paper cover, containing notanda and sententiæ notabiles from various alchemical authors. Greater part blank.

2. A list of chemical authors.

3. Several Indices Chemici.

4. De peste. Van Helmont.

5. Note as to Terra lemna, and Terra sigillata, with Leibnitz's address.

6. List of books on Chemistry with shelf-marks (perhaps in Trinity Library).

7. An alchemical recipe headed " Roth Mallor's work." On the back of the folio a recipe for making aqua regia from calcium chloride and aqua fortis, and for another menstruum which seems to be a solution of antimony chloride. The 2nd Period (a part of the foregoing recipe), but not in Newton's hand.

8. Notes of reference to some alchemical works. Diagrams of furnaces. Sundry recipes for making clay for furnaces and lutes. Note that " for rectifying spirits and ethereal oyles, nothing is better than the bladder of an ox or hogg," and a recipe for calcining gold which seems only getting it into a fine powder.

9. Dr Goddard's experiments of refining gold with antimony, extracted from Phil. Trans.

10. Part of a letter ordering some one to procure for Newton from Hamburg various metallic ores. On the back a note about something being true when angles due to difference of refraction are taken small enough, and a recipe for some plaster.

(5)

1. Anagrams of "Isaacus Newtonus" on draft of a letter to the Council about some matter at the Mint. Note of quotations in ludo puerorum, scala philosophorum, and rosario.

2. Directions as to some details of an alchemical process given by a Londoner acquainted with Mr Boyle and Dr Dickinson. On the back the beginning of a letter in which mention is made of Mr Pepys asking Sir I. N. for a method of finding the longitude at sea.

3. List of Alchemical works. A classification of the same with dates. On the back an account of gold and silver moneys coined since Christmas (no year), in which the guinea is put at 21s. 6d.

4. Another list of Alchemical authors with dates.

5. Another list of Alchemical authors, with extracts from Act of Parl. 5 Car. II., on coinage, on the back.

6. Extracts "ex lumine de tenebris."

7. A treatise on Chemistry, extracted from various authors, similar to nos. 18, 31, above ; with some odd papers partly duplicates.

8. Two chapters apparently of another such treatise, headed "Reductio et sublimatio" (2 fol.), and "Separatio elementorum" (1 fol.) compiled as before.

9. Recipes for cements. Address of 2 stampmakers. Mathematical diagrams and lists of alchemical works.

10. Opus Galli Anonymi. With a note by Newton "Simile est hoc opus operi Fabri..." It gives a recipe for the Philosopher's stone and medicine but it does not state what the material operated on is ; the preparation consists in repeated digestions and distillations.

11. Alchemical operations—references to the pages of several books.

12. Experimenta Raymundi (2 fol.).

13. Observationes (heads of Alchemical process).

14. Ex Fabri Hydrographo Spagyrico (1 f.).

15. Ex Hercule prochymico (1 f.).

16. Miscellanea from Raymund and others (1 f.).

17. The Regimen, in seven aphorisms and notes thereon (2 f.).

18. Index chemicus (commencement only).

19. Various extracts from alchemical works (9 f.).

N.   2

20. Out of 'La Lumière sortant des Ténèbres' [above, no. 6], and commentary thereon (1 f.), but incomplete.

21. Fragment out of some treatise with pictures—no beginning or end.

22. Recipes for lutes, with some addresses on the back.

23. Recipes for some alchemical medicines, with address of a druggist.

24. Other alchemical operations, one a translation, and one not in Newton's hand.

25. Abstract of Yarworth's " Processus "—incomplete, extending to Chap. v.

26. An alchemical tract entitled " Manna," not in Newton's hand, but with additions and notes at the end in his hand.

27. Recipe for Regulus Martis; on the back some arithmetical calculation.

28. Copy (not in Newton's handwriting) of a letter from Mr John Casswell, Oxford, Oct. 14, 1694, to Mr John Flamsteed, giving an account of some observations on magnetism.

29. Account of a method for making aqua fortis and for refining silver, in Conduitt's hand.

30. " Experimentum Bellini."

31. Theatrum Astronomiæ Terrestris.

---

*II.

Packet marked VI. containing the following papers on Alchemy :

1. Some alchemical receipts, not in Newton's hand.

2. Queries, not in Newton's hand.

3. A medicine to transmute copper, ditto.

4. Alchemical receipts, ditto.

5. To make artificial pearl, ditto.

*III.

Two bound MS. copies of Yarworth's "Processus," both incomplete.
A MS. book on Alchemy, containing

The apocalyps or revelation of the secret spirit, by an unknown author.

Quotations from divers writers on alchemy.

An unknown author upon the philosopher's stone.

Ex epistolâ Johannis pauperis.

De Alkymiæ veritate   δε Λαπιδιβυς &c.

The breefe of Sir Edward Vere's book.   Aug. 18, 1610.

IV. NOTES OF EXPERIMENTS, ALL IN NEWTON'S HAND.

1. Dec. 10. 1678 to Jan. 15. Subliming antimony with salammoniac. Alloying antimony with lead and other metals. (No definite
result of value.)

2. Jan. 1679—80. Subliming antimonial sublimate with lead
antimoniate &c. Jan. 22. Action of nitric acid and salammoniac on
antimony sulphide &c. and further sublimations. (Most of these
experiments are roughly quantitative.)   •

3. Feb. 1679—80. Fusing antimony with vitriol and other
things. Sublimation of various metals by help of antimony and
salammoniac &c. Action of oil of vitriol on galena, of nitric acid
on sublimate of antimony, and others of a like kind.

4. Aug. 1682. Similar experiments; some on lead ore, others
on an alloy of tin and bismuth which he seems to call Diana.

5. July 10 (no year), "vidi ✳philosophicum." Sublimations of
calx albus with salammoniac.

6. April 26, 1686. On a volatile salt of zinc (apparently the
chloride), and on an alloy derived from ores of iron, antimony, tin,
lead, and bismuth. May 16. "On ven. vol."

7. Mar. 5, 1690—1 and Mar. 16. On some bismuth compounds
and the action of aqua fortis on alloys of tin and bismuth and zinc.

8. Experiments and observations, Dec. 1692 and Jan. 1692—3.
Working of barm. He says "in distilling new wine before fermentation, the flegm rises first, and then the spirit, but after fermentation,
the spirit rises before the flegm." Other experiments. Comparison of
the fusibility of alloys of lead, tin, and bismuth, in which is given

2—2

as the most fusible an alloy of 5 of lead + 7 of tin + 12 of bismuth. April 1693 and June 1693, further experiments.

9.   April 1695.   Experiments with antimony and ores of iron, copper, and tin, and sublimations with salammoniac.   Feb. 1695—6, sublimations of antimony with iron ore.

10.   Notes of Chemical Experiments, without date:

Action of aqua fortis on antimony sulphide, &c.

Sublimation of alloy of antimony and lead with salammoniac, &c.

Experiments on lead ore and other things.

Do. on copper &c.

Other experiments.

11.   De metallo ad conficiendum speculum componendo et fundendo.   Printed by Brewster, ii. 535.

V.   Miscellaneous Notes.

1.   Notes on Magnetism.   It does not appear whence they are taken.   The observations (some of which are erroneous) do not seem to be Newton's, though here and there remarks upon them seem to be his.

2.   De Natura Acidorum, with a copy.   This is printed in Horsley's Newton, iv. pp. 397—400.

3.   Eleven points for enquiry in Physics.

4.   De Gemmis in genere, notes, mostly from Berquen, Boethius, Tavernier, and Boyle.   Index of refraction in diamonds is given $\frac{41}{100}$ on the authority of Halley.   On p. 3 is mentioned a very fragile and soft western Topaz which he found to have a specific gravity 4.27, though the sines of refraction were as 14 to 23 (could this be Baryte?).   On p. 7 he deduces from the cleavage that gems are crystallized like salts from juices which turn to stone.   At the end are the gold and silver standards of different countries.

5.   De Gemmis.   Other notes mostly included in the preceding, but on p. 1 are given reasons for thinking the diamond coagulated from a fluid and fat substance, which he does not seem to have incorporated in the preceding.

VI.   A Manuscript Note-Book

containing

On the fly-leaf—Notes of the value, hardness and other qualities of gems.

pp. 1 to 22, of colours.   Articles 1—5 from Boyle's experiments and considerations touching colour, 1664.

Arts. 6 to 21, experiments with prisms; 22 and 26 on internal reflection at or near the critical angle ; 27 to 43 on effects of thin plates of air between glasses.

44—47, further experiments with prisms ; 48, colours from admixture; 49, reflection at two contiguous surfaces of glass ; 50, colours of thin plates of glass, soap-bubbles, &c. ; 51—53, on colours by internal reflection in spheres of water ; 54, effect of oblique rays on the size of the spot at contact of 2 glasses ; 55, diminished reflection of glass in water ; 56 and 57, light reflected from powders, &c. ; 58—62, effects of distorting the eye-ball ; 63, coloured impressions of objects remaining when the eye is no longer directed to them ; 64, on the action of the retina and optic nerve (quoted by Brewster i. 432 from Harris, omitting the last paragraph), and on p. 22, notes of the thickness of vibrations of light.

p. 22, notes from Boyle on increased sensitiveness of sight and hearing produced by sickness.   Of vegetable substances precipitating vitriol black.

p. 23, a receipt for ink.

pp. 25—41, extracts from Boyle "on the mechanical origin of Heat and Cold," Oxford, 1675. The observations on p. 25 as to the expansion of glass, and those on the elasticity of springs are not in Boyle on Heat and Cold. The book quoted in the MS. is called the "History of Cold," which is not the title of the 1675 edition, but forms part of the title in the collected works.

p. 45, quotations from Boyle. Some incomplete trials of the height at which a thermometer stands in several substances—melting wax, tin, lead, &c. on Mar. 10, 1692—3. An experiment for determining the expansion of air by heat, also that of linseed oil (Brewster, ii. 366).

p. 49, extracts from Boyle's new experiments touching the spring of the air.   At the bottom of this page and on

p. 50, account of experiments on flame—with conclusion that flame and vapour differ only as bodies red-hot and not red-hot.

p. 51, guesses heat to be made by division of parts, for when two particles are parted it makes the æther rush in betwixt them and so vibrate.   Receipt for making Phosphorus (Brandt's).

pp. 53—60, blank ; pp. 61—65, extracts from Boyle on formes.

p. 65, extracts from Starkey's Pyrotechny asserted.

p. 66, note of a petrifying spring in Peru, from a Spanish treatise translated, by the Earl of Sandwich.

pp. 57—70, blank ; pp. 71—80, extracts from Boyle on formes.

p. 80, experiments on the extraction of mercury from the nitrate and from corrosive sublimate by various other metals.

pp. 81, 82, receipts for making regulus of antimony by different metals.

p. 83, notes of alloys which fuse at low temperatures, and others which give a crystalline mass from fusion.   Notes of the action of aquafortis, and of salammoniac, on salt, and oil of tartar or potassium carbonate; and of crude tartar on the same, and of tartarum vitriolatum (potassium bisulphate) on same : with

p. 84, the remark that some *fools* call the result of the last reaction magisterium tartari vitriolati.

note, that salammoniac is less volatile than muriatic acid or ammonium carbonate, which seems to explain a quotation from D. von der Becke which follows.

note of calcination of lead with salt of antimony and salammoniac and of volatilization of arsenical tin when heated with corrosive sublimate and salammoniac.

pp. 85—92, extracts from Boyle.

pp. 93—100, sundry receipts and extracts on various chemical reactions, chiefly from Boyle.

p. 101, receipts for making sundry preparations of antimony. Note of the action of corrosive sublimate on various ores.

p. 102, notes of experiments in the preparation of regulus of saturation of spirit of antimony by different substances has blanks left for the quantities.

pp. 106, 107, other chemical experiments. Note of composition of fusible metal " which in summer will melt in the sun," with the (erroneous) remark that tinglas is more fusible than tin.

pp. 108—112, chemical experiments chiefly on preparations of antimony and scoria of regulus. Some of these (e.g. p. 111) are marked with an N in the margin.

p. 113, action of distilled liquor of antimony on salts of lead, iron and copper; action of heat on tartarised antimony.

p. 114, action of spar on distilled liquor of antimony, vinegar, and aquafortis, and of salt from clay of lead mines on do.; action of nitre on antimony.

pp. 115, 116, action of oil of vitriol on lead ore, and of an antimonial sublimate on several substances.

pp. 117—120, experiments with a substance to which the name " ven. vol." is given.

p. 121, note, that on May 10, 1681, and on the 14th and 15th he comprehended sundry alchemical names. This note has been scratched out, apparently in consequence of its having nothing to do with the subject of the other notes, but it is not certain that the foregoing experiments have not something to do with it.

p. 122, another note, that on May 18 he completed the solution of the alchemical symbol of the caduceus, followed by experiments on June 10 on sublimation of green and blue vitriol with salammoniac and the resulting sublimate with lead ore. Perhaps these experiments on sublimation were designed to test his interpretation of some alchemical symbols.

pp. 123 sqq. to 126, account of experiments in May and June, 1682; on sublimation of some salts with salammoniac, and some metals and alloys with the same, and with antimony.

pp. 127 to 130, June 26, 1682, and July 4, 1682, account of experiments on obtaining regulus from mixture of lead ores, antimony and bismuth; and others similar.

p. 131, experiments on the action of various reguluses with spirit (? of salt).

pp. 132—4, other experiments on sublimation—the date, Tuesday, July 19, is given on p. 133; this must have been in 1683.

pp. 135 sqq., Feb. 29, 1683—4. An experiment in which he prepared the chlorides of mercury.

pp. 140 sqq., further experiments on "the net" which seems to contain iron and copper, and others of a similar kind.   On p. 149 is the date, Friday, May 23.

p. 150, experiments on the spirit of zinc, Apr. 26, 1686.

pp. 151 to 158, experiments on some alloys of copper, antimony and iron, and continued on p. 267.

pp. 159 to 193, extracts from Boyle on the medical virtues of saline and other preparations.

pp. 194 to 206, blank; p. 207, extracts from Boyle on volatile salts of animal and vegetable substances.

pp. 209—223, extracts from Starkey's Pyrotechny asserted—on alkalies.

pp. 224 to 242, blank, except some headings.

pp. 243—4, some extracts from "Secrets Revealed" and other alchemical works.

pp. 245 to 260, blank, except heading.

p. 261, some references to alchemical works.   pp. 262—4, blank.

p. 265, recipe for ether, and its uses in medicine.

p. 266, some recipes for medicines.

pp. 267, 8, continuation of experiments from p. 158.   On this page is mentioned a liquor which dissolves the tinctures out of gold, silver, &c. and leaves only a white calx—but no directions for preparing it.   Further experiments.

pp. 269—283, on regulus of antimony and alloys; similar in character to the former : rest of book. blank, except 3 pages at end, where is a list of prices of some chemicals in 1687 and again in 1693, and some notes of sublimation of vitriol with salammoniac.

*SECTION III.

CHRONOLOGY.

1. Chapter v. of the Chronology of Ancient Kingdoms amended. A description of the Temple of Solomon. (Horsley's Newton, v. pp. 236 seqq.)

2. Transcript of part of the work on Chronology.

3. Considerations about rectifying the Julian Calendar.

4. Considerations about the Julian Calendar.

5. On the Chronology of the Egyptians, of the Gospel, &c. (confused).

6. Seven drafts (all in Newton's hand) of his remarks on the Chronology published under his name at Paris.

7. Some notes on the "Chronologie Abrégée."

8. Dedication (in French) of Newton's Chronology to the Queen.

*SECTION IV.

HISTORY.

Papers on various historical subjects, chiefly of the reign of James II., relating to the Father Francis business, &c.

1. Certain arguments collected out of the Scriptures, out of the Civill Law, and the Common, exhibited to the Queen's Majestie by some of both houses against the Queen of Scots. Anno 13 Elizabeth.

2. An instance of Queen Elizabeth's power of dispensing with Acts of Parliament offered to the consideration of the Gentlemen of the University of Cambridge.

3. An argument perswading that the Queen's Majestie ought to have in conscience a great care of the safety of her own person.

4. A copy of the association and Act of Parliament enforcing it in the reign of Queen Elizabeth.

5. Royal Commission of James II. for a search and examination into the statutes of the Universities, Cathedral bodies, Grammar Schools, and other Ecclesiastical corporations.

6. The answer of the Vice-chancellor and Senate of the University of Cambridge to the question why they did not admit Alban Francis to the degree of M. A.

7. The answer to some questions propounded by the Lord Chancellor at the appearance of the Vice-chancellor and deputies of the Senate of the University of Cambridge before the Lords Commissioners. May 7, 1687. (5 copies.)

10. An apology for the Church of England with relation to the spirit of persecution for which she is accused.

11. A letter of the Rev. F. Peter Jesuite, Almoner to the King of England, written to the Rev. F. le Chaise, confessor to the most Christian King, touching the present affairs of England. (2 copies.)

12. Copie d'une lettre d'un Jesuite de Leige écrit a un Jesuite de Friburge, le 2 Fevr. 1687. In Latin. (2 copies.)

13. The draft of an act for the better prevention of illegal exaction of money from the subject and preservation of the right and freedom of the subjects of this realm.

14. Notes of an argument in the case of Godden versus Sir Edw. Hales. 16 June, 1686.

15. The answer of the Fellows of S. Mary Magdalen College, [Oxford], to the question why they did not elect and admit Mr. Anthony Farmer to be President of the same College in the room of Dr. Clarke deceased, in complyance with his Majesties Letters mandatory.

16. The attempt of Dr. Fairfax to be heard before the commissioners, June 13, 1687. Followed by a second draft of the answer of the Vice-President and other Fellows of S. Mary Magdalen, Oxon., and a piece of a letter to the E. of Sunderland.

17. Reasons for subscribing the Oxford Address by the Clergy of the diocese.

18. 14 Directions in aid of the king's government.

19. Notes upon the dispensing power.

20. The case of the Bishops' courts.

21. A series of extracts from the Decretals, &c. "Principis mandata contemnentes quomodo puniantur."

22. A paper beginning, "His Majesties promise is no argument for abrogating the Laws." On the other side, some "Rules" respecting Acts for Liberty of Conscience, Election of Parliaments, &c.

23. Some queries concerning liberty of conscience directed to William Penn and Henry Care.

24. The petition of the seven Bishops. (3 copies.)

25. Notes out of the Diary of the Parliament, 1660.

26.   Address of the Lord-Lieutenant, Gentlemen, and Freeholders of the County of Cambridge to William of Orange.

27.   The Bishop of London's Protestation.

28.   The Bishop of London's narrative of the proceedings against him before the High Commissioners, August, 1686.

29.   Letter of Newton to ————, 19 Feb. 1687-8, on the mandamus to admit Father Francis to M.A.

30.   Notes of Egyptian mythology, out of Plutarch.
      do.   do.   Theology, from various authors.
      Mythological notes,   do. (3 f.).

31.   The original of Monarchies, chapter I.

32.   Antiquarian Fragments.
      On the Tyrrhenians, &c.

·*SECTION V.

1.   The question stated about abstaining from Blood, in Newton's hand.

2.   Prophecies concerning Christ's second coming, chiefly a collection of texts, followed by some extracts from the Talmud, &c., in five sheets: all in Newton's hand.

3.   Irenicum, or Ecclesiastical Polyty tending to peace.   Two separate drafts, both in Newton's hand.   Part printed by Brewster, ii. 526.

4.   Quæres regarding the word ὁμοουσίος.   Printed by Brewster, ii. 532.

5.   Extract by Newton Ex Marci Maximi Cæsaraugustani in Hispaniis Episcopi Chronico.

6.   Draft in Newton's hand on the rise of the Apostasy in point of religion.

7.   Chronological notes, notes on the site of the seven churches of Asia, &c., in Newton's hand.

8.   Extracts by Newton "out of Cudworth," two sheets.

9.   Profession of faith by Roman Bishops and Presbyters.

10.   Loose papers with notes on the Prophecies, and other Theological notes and extracts, with some relating to Chronology, almost all in Newton's hand.

11.   Paradoxical questions concerning the morals and actions of Athanasius and his followers.   All in Newton's hand.   Partly printed by Brewster, ii. 342.

12.   A collection of papers, apparently being the draft of a work on "Religion," the chapters headed "a short scheme of the true religion," "of the religion of the Jews and Christians," "of the rise of the R. C. church in ecclesiastical dominion."   All in Newton's hand.   Brewster, ii. p. 347.

13. Note in Newton's hand, "God made and governs the world, &c." Printed by Brewster, ii. 354.

14. A sermon on 2 Kings xvii. 15, 16, in Newton's hand.

15. Lexici Prophetici pars secunda, in quibus agitur De forma sanctuarii Judaici. This is a treatise in Latin on the Temple of Solomon.

16. Miscellaneous extracts from Maimonides, Irenæus adversus hæreses, and some notes partly mythological.

17. (1), (2), (3). Three drafts of the observations on the Prophecies of Holy Writ, written on loose sheets, backs of letters, &c.

(1) Contains also two sheets of Spicilegia variantium lectionum in Apocalypsi.

(2) Contains also various observations on the way of printing the book.

(3) Contains also a Synopsis of the Synchronism of the Apocalypse.

18. Some chapters of the work on the Corruption of religion, the Host of Heaven, &c.

19. A bundle containing

(1) Collections for the work on the Prophecies.

(2) A treatise divided into chapters against the R. C. Church.

(3) Attempt to form a universal language. This contains also a genealogical tree of the Newton family, and at the other end an English and Latin phrase-book, not in N.'s hand.

(4) A treatise in Latin on the "Tuba quarta" of the Apocalypse.

20. Corruptelæ duorum celebrium in sacris literis locorum historica narratio; vid. 1 John v. 7, 1 Tim. iii. 16. Amstelædami, 1709.

This is a Latin version of the first part of the "Historical account of two notable corruptions of Scripture," published in the 5th volume of Horsley's Newton, p. 495. It is not in Newton's hand, but contains a few corrections by him. Though the title speaks of two texts, it only treats of the first: it is however complete, ending with *finis*. It is rather fuller than the English treatise, *e.g.* the Slavonick

22.   Several chapters of the work on the Church, its corruptions, &c., with three drafts of a table of contents.

23.   On the language of the Prophecies—paged—perfect.

24.   On the Origin of all religion, with other chapters of the Theological works (imperfect).

25.   Transcript of part of a work on the Prophecies, paged from 25 to 173, imp. at both ends.

26.   Variantes Lectiones Apocalypticæ.

27.   Latin Theological Treatises, all imperfect.

28.   A bundle containing
    (1)   Introductio continens Apocalypseos rationem generalem.
    (2)   Prœmium historiæ ecclesiasticæ.
    (3)   De monachismo.
    (4)   Historia de concilio Nicen.
    (5)   A treatise beginning "Fidei vero formula," &c.
    (6)   Extr. ex Sibyllinorum oraculis.
These are all perfect.
    (7)   De annis prædicationis Christi (imperfect).

29.   Rough drafts of some of the chapters of the work on the Prophecies.

30.   Some chapters of the treatise on " The working of the mystery of Iniquity," " the Host of Heaven," &c.

31.   Of the original of pious frauds.   Paradoxical questions— in a wretched state.

32.   The synchronism of the three parts of the prophetick interpretation, with other loose sheets on the prophecies.

33.   Several chapters of the work on the Prophecies, written out fairly for the press, others not included in that work.

34.   On the Papacy and the prophecies relating thereto.

35.   Loose papers concerning worship, the Irenicum, &c.

36.   Preparations in English and Latin for the work on the Revelation : hopelessly confused.

37.   A treatise on the Revelation in English, imperfect, with several copies of parts.   The beginning (containing the introduction) is complete.

38.   Miscellaneous Theological notes and extracts.

39.   Theologiæ Gentilis Origines Philosophicæ.

40.   Theological scraps.

SECTION VI.

LETTERS.

I.

CORRESPONDENCE WITH OLDENBURG.

Oldenburg to Newton, Jan. 18, 1672.
Newton to Oldenburg, March 26, 1672.
 ,, ,, · March 30, 1672.
Oldenburg to Newton, Early in April, 1672.
Newton to Oldenburg, April 13, 1672, in reply to the above.
Oldenburg to Newton, May 2, 1672.
Newton to Oldenburg, May 4, 1672.
 ,, ,, May 21, 1672.
Oldenburg to Newton, July 2, 1672.
Newton to Oldenburg, July 11, 1672.
Oldenburg to Newton, Sept. 24, 1672.
 ,, ,, June 4, 1673.
 .. ,, June 7, 1673.
 ,, ,, Sept. 14, 1673.
Newton to Oldenburg, Feb. 19, 1676.
 ,, .. Sept. 2, 1676, Brewster, i. 129. On
      planting cyder-trees, with a copy.
 ,, ,, Nov. 28, 1676.
Oldenburg to Newton, Jan. 2, 1677.

II.

CORRESPONDENCE WITH COLLINS AND WALLIS.

Copy of Newton's letters to Oldenburg, dated June 13 and Oct. 24, 1676, made for Wallis.

Another copy, somewhat mutilated, of the same letters.

Draft of Newton's letter to Wallis about them.

Draft of a later letter to Wallis containing corrections to typographical errors in Wallis's printed account of Newton's method in Vol. 2, and Newton's remarks on his own and Leibnitz's letters printed in Vol. 3.

Wallis to Newton, April 10, 1695. Copy. Edleston, p. 300.

..   ,,   April 30, 1695. Published in Brewster, Vol. ii. p. 427.

,,   May 30, 1695.

..   ,,   July 3, 1695.

,,   July 1, 1695, on Leibnitz's letter of 28 May. Brewster, ii. 429.

,,   ,,   Jan. 9, 1698–9.

Extract of two letters from Wallis concerning a change in the Calendar, June 13, 30, 1699.

III.

LETTERS FROM ARTHUR STORER TO Dr BABINGTON AND TO NEWTON,

Containing some Astronomical Tables, and Communications respecting the Comets of 1680 and 1682.

Arthur Storer to Mr Newton, Boothby, Aug. 10, 1678, with Table showing hourly Altitude and Azimuth of the " North Star."

Arthur Storer to Mr Newton, London, Sept. 4, 1678, with Table of the Sun's Azimuth.

Arthur Storer to Dr Babington; London, Sept. 19, 1678.

Arthur Storer to Dr Babington, Oct. 1, 1678, with an Astronomical Table "to find the Sun or any Star's Altitude," &c.

Arthur Storer to Dr Babington, from Patuxant River in Maryland, April 18, 1681, about the Comet of 1680 as observed in Maryland.

Arthur Storer to Mr Isaac Newton, from Patuxant River in Maryland, April 26, 1683, with observations of a Comet which appeared in Maryland, Aug. 14, 1682, till Sept. 12, 1682.

IV.

CORRESPONDENCE WITH FLAMSTEED.

Flamsteed to Newton,	Dec. 15, 1680.
Flamsteed to Crompton (for Newton)	March 7, 1680–1,

with an extract in Newton's hand from a letter of Flamsteed dated Feb. 12th, 1680–1.

Newton to Flamsteed,	April 12, 1681.
Draft'of Newton to Flamsteed,	April 16, 1681, pr. by Brewster, ii. 455.

Draft of Newton to Flamsteed Canterbury, Dec. 29th, } imperfect.　Dec. 29, 1681.

The above all relate to the comet of 1680.

Flamsteed to Newton,		Dec. 27, 1684.
..	..	Jan. 5, 1684–5.
		Jan. 27, 1684–5.
		Sept. 26, 1685.
..	,,	Oct. 10, 1685.
,,	,,	Sept. 9, 1686.
Flamsteed to Mr Glen,		April 10, 1693. Concerning earthquakes. Copy made for Newton, with ·a note concerning Flamsteed's star-maps.
Flamsteed to Newton,		Sept. 7, 1694.
..	..	Oct. 11, 1694. (Printed in Baily's Flamsteed, p. 134.)
		Oct. 25, 1694.
		Oct. 29, 1694.
		Nov. 3, 1694.
		Nov. 27, 1694.
		Dec. 10, 1694.
		Dec. 31, 1694.
		Jan. 18, 1694–5.
		Jan. 29, 1694–5.
		Feb. 7, 1694–5.
		March 2, 1694–5.
		March 21, 1694–5.
		April 20, 1695.

Flamsteed to Newton,   July 13, 1695.

..   ..   July 18, 1695.

                July 23, 1695.

                Aug. 4, 1695.

                Aug. 6, 1695.

                Sept. 19, 1695.

                Jan. 11, 1696.

                Sept. 4, 1697.

                Dec. 10, 1697.

                Dec. 29, 1698.   Note by Flamsteed of the no. of observations of planets taken between 1675 and 1689.

Flamsteed to Dr Wallis,   Dec. 20, 1698.   Printed copy of Latin letter.

Flamsteed to Newton,   Jan. 2, 1698–9.

V.

GREGORY TO NEWTON.

David Gregory to Newton,   June 9, 1684.

              ,,   Sept. 2, 1684.

              ,,   August 27, 1691.

..   ,,   Oct. 10, 1691.

              ,,   Nov. 7, 1691.

              ,,   Nov. 7, 1691.

              ,,   Nov. 26, 1691.

              ,,   Sept. 24, 1694.

              ,,   Dec. 23, 1697.

,,   ,,   Sept. 30, 1702.

Newton to Gregory (draft), no date, about 1691.

VI.

LETTERS FROM HALLEY TO NEWTON RELATING TO THE PUBLICATION OF THE FIRST EDITION OF THE 'PRINCIPIA.'

May 22, 1686.   Printed in Brewster's Life of Newton,

                      Append. 8 & 12 to Vol. i. p. 438

June 29, 1686.   ,,   ,,   ,,   p. 446

June 7, 1686.   Printed in Brewster's Life of Newton,
         Append. 8 & 12 to Vol. i. p. 472
Oct. 14, 1686.   ,,   ,, ..   p. 473
Feb. 24, 1686–7. ,,   p. 474
March 7, 1686–7. ,,   p. 475
March 14, 1686–7. ,,   p. 476
April 5, 1687.   ,,   p. 477
July, 5, 1687.   Vol. ii. p. 111

VII.

HALLEY TO NEWTON ABOUT COMETS' ORBITS.

Halley to Newton, Sept. 7, 1695.
  ,,   ,, Sept. 28, 1695.
        early in Oct. 1695.
   ..   Oct. 15, 1695, with observations of a Comet
        May 1665.
Newton to Halley, Oct. 17, 1695, with draft of same letter.
Halley to Newton, Oct. 21, 1695.
Draft of a letter by Newton to Halley.
Halley to Newton, Feb. 16, 1725.
Newton to Halley, March 1, 1725, with draft of same letter.
A calculation of Halley relating to the Comet of 1680—on a
separate sheet.

*VIII.

HALLEY TO NEWTON AND MOLYNEUX, RELATING
TO THE CHESTER MINT.

Halley to Newton, Nov. 28, 1696.
  ,,   .. Feb. 13, 1697.
  ,,   ,, August 2, 1697.
  ,,   ,, Dec. 30, 1697.
Halley to Molyneux, July 21, 1697.

IX.

COTES'S LETTERS TO NEWTON, MOSTLY PUBLISHED IN EDLESTON'S CORRESPONDENCE OF NEWTON AND COTES,

Together with three Letters and a Memorandum by Robert Smith relating to the foregoing letters and the publication of Cotes's works.

Cotes to Newton. April 29, 1715, On the Eclipse of the Sun, 22nd April, partly given in Edleston, p. 179.

Robert Smith to Newton, relating to the publication of Cotes's works, Dec. 23, 1718; Aug. 12, 1720.

Robert Smith to John Conduitt, Esqʳᵉ., Feb. 4, 1732—3, asking for the loan to him of the foregoing letter of Cotes on the Eclipse.

Also a memorandum dated June 6, 1738, acknowledging the receipt of certain letters of Cotes to Newton lent to him by Mrs Conduitt.

X.

ROUGH DRAFTS OF SOME OF NEWTON'S LETTERS TO COTES.

The letters in Edleston and the pages to which these drafts relate are given in the following list:

This is rather fuller than the letter printed by Edleston.

XI.

KEILL TO NEWTON.

Keill to Newton,   April 3, 1711.

Copy of Keill's answer to the letter "pro eminente Mathematico," in the Journal Littéraire, 29th July, 1713.

Keill to Newton,   Nov. 9, 1713.

„   „   Feb. 8, 1713-4. ⁄ Answer in Edleston, *Correspondence of Newton and Cotes*, p. 169, dated April 2.

Johnson to Keill,   Feb. 9, 1713-4.

Keill to Newton,   April 20, 1714.   Answer in Edleston, p. 170.

„   „   May 2, 1714.

„   „   May 14, 1714.

(Draft of a letter from Newton to Keill dated May 15, 1714, is printed in Edleston, p. 176.)

Keill to Newton,   May 17, 1714.

„   „   May 21, 1714.

„   „   May 25, 1714.   ··

„   „   June 2, 1714.

„   „   June 24, 1714. ·

„   „   Aug. 6, 1714.

„   „   Oct. 29, 1715.

„   „   Nov. 10, 1715.

„   „   May 17, 1717.

„   „   May 23, 1718.

(On the back of Keill's letter of Oct. 29, 1715, there is a scrap in Newton's hand in answer to an objection of Bernouilli.)

XII.

PEMBERTON'S LETTERS TO NEWTON WHILE EDITING THE 3RD EDITION OF THE 'PRINCIPIA.'

Pemberton to Newton,   Feb. 11, 1723-4. ·

„   „   Feb. 18, 1723-4.

„   „   May 17, 1725.

„   „   Monday, May 31, 1725.

„   „   Tuesday Morning, June 22, 1725.

„   „   July 17, 1725.

„   „   Feb. 9, 1725-6.

Besides these, 16 undated letters and 7 sheets of queries.

*XIII.

LETTERS FROM N. FACIO DUILLIER
TO NEWTON AND OTHERS.

N. Facio Duillier to Newton,   Nov. 17, 1692.

..   ..   Nov. 22, 1692.

                                     May 4, 1693.

        ,,   ,,   June 15, 1717.

        ,,   ,,   April 1, 1724.

N. Facio Duillier to Conduitt, Aug. 8, 1730 (with proposed Epitaphs on Newton).

N. Facio Duillier to Conduitt,   Aug. 12, 1730.

        ,,   ,,   Aug. 26, 1730.

Abstract of Facio's Letter to Dr Worth, Jan. 26, 1731–2.

N. Facio Duillier to Conduitt,   April 5, 1732.

                                     April 10, 1732.

        ,,   April 12, 1732, with enclosed petition to the king.

Petition to the Commons.

A printed copy of a Latin Eclogue on Newton by M. Facio de Duillier.

---

*XIV.

MISCELLANEOUS LETTERS.

1. Venan(?) to Huyghens, Aug. 20, 1664.

2. Borellius to Wallis (Latin), Dec. 6, 1670.

3. Collins to Borellius, Junii 8, 1672.

4. Robert Hooke to Newton, Feb. 1675—6. Brewster, i. 140.

5. Newton to Hook (on thin plates), Feb. 5, 1675—6. Brewster, i. 141.

6. Thomas Burnet to Newton, Jan. 13, 1680–81.

10. Gilbert Clerke to Newton, on difficulties in the Principia, 26 Sept. 1687, with draft of Newton's answer.

Gilbert Clerke to Newton, Oct. 3, 1687.

„　　　„　　　　„　　Nov. 7, 1687.

„　　　„　　　　„　　Nov. 21, 1687.

11. John Locke to Newton, July 26 [1692]. Brewster, ii. 461.

12. Richard Bentley to Newton, Feb. 18, 1692–3. Brewster, ii. 463.

13. John Mill to Newton, Nov. 7, 1693. Brewster, ii. 472.

14. Samuel Pepys to Newton, Dec. 21, 1693. Brewster, ii. 471.

15. Nath. Hawes to Newton, May 29, 1694.

16. Basnage de Bonval to Newton, Aug. 22 (no year), De la Haye.

17. Charles Montague to Newton, March 19, 1695 (offering the mastership of the Mint). Brewster, ii. 191.

18. Cassini to Newton, April 6, 1698, on the Satellites of Saturn.

19. Truchet to Newton (no date), acknowledgment of a copy of Newton's Optics translated into French.

20. T. Horne to Newton, Aug. 22 (no year).

21. John Hockett to Newton, Sept. 14, 1699 (asking interest for his son at Trinity, with some chron. notes of Newton on the back).

22. ——————— to Lady Norris, proposing marriage (copy in Conduitt's hand), 1703—4. Brewster, ii. 211.

23. Lord Halifax to Newton, March 17 [1704—5]. Brewster, ii. 216.

24. Lord Halifax to Newton, May 5, 1705. Brewster, ii. 217.

25, 26. Two drafts of Newton's letter to a friend at Cambridge, about the election [1705]. Brewster, ii. 215.

27. Draft of part of a letter from Newton to [F. Godolphin?] [1705.]

28. D. Gregory to Newton, Sept. 16, 1707, about the Scottish coinage.

29. R. Bentley to Newton, June 10, 1708. Brewster, ii. 248.

30. 　　„　　　　„　　Oct. 20, 1709. Brewster, ii. 250.

31. Remond de Monmort to Newton, Feb. 16, 1709–10.

32. 　„　　„　　„　　to Newton, giving an account of the quarrel between Drs Sloane and Woodward, about stones in the gall-bladder, March 28, 1711. Brewster, ii. 244.

33. J. Derham to Newton, Feb. 20, 1712—3. Brewster, ii. 519.

34. R. Bentley to Newton, July 1 [1713].   Brewster, ii. 254.

35. The Abbé Bignon to Newton, Nov. 30, 1713.

36, 37. Draft of a letter from Newton to the Abbé Bignon, with a copy by Conduitt.

38. Varignon to Newton, Dec. 5, 1713.

39. R. Bentley to Newton, Jan. 6, 1713–4.

40. .'J. Derham to Newton, about his physico-theology, May 11, 1714 (with some notes by Newton on Osiris, the length of the year, etc.).

41. John Chamberlayne to Newton, May 20, 1714.

42. Fontenelle to Newton, June 9, 1714.

43. A. Menzikoff to Newton, asking admission to the Royal Society, Aug. 23, 1714.

44. Three drafts of Newton's answer, Oct. 21, 1714.

45. John Chamberlayne to Newton, Oct. 28, 1714.

46.   ,,   ,,   ,,   ,,   (no date) Friday morning.

47. Varignon to Newton, Nov. 18, 1714.

48. Fontenelle to Newton, Feb. 4, 1714—5. Brewster, ii. 518.

49. Sir Alex. Cunningham to Newton, Feb. 21, 1716. Venice.

50. Draft of letter from Newton to Bernouilli about the omission of his name from the list of Fellows of the Royal Society.

51. Brook Taylor to Newton, April 22, 1716. Brewster, ii. 509.

52 Sir Alex. Cunningham to Newton, May 1, 1716. Venice.

53. Conti to Newton, Dec. 10, 1716. Brewster, ii. 434.

54. Letter of Remond de Montmort to Newton, dated Paris, Feb. 25, 1716–7.

55. John Bernouilli to R. de Monmort, Apr. 8, 1717 (copy, with an addition by Newton). Brewster, ii. 437.

56. Nich. Bernouilli to Newton, May 31, 1717.

57. Fontenelle to Chamberlayne, July 6, 1717 (extract in Mrs Barton's hand). Brewster, ii. 289.

58. Remond de Monmort to Newton, March 27, 1718.

59. Letter from Brook Taylor to Mr Innys, dated Aug. 12,

61. Varignon to Newton, Nov. 17, 1718.

62. Remond de Monmort to Taylor, Dec. 18, 1718. (Copy.) Brewster, ii. 511.

63. Varignon to Newton, July 26, 1719.

64. Newton to Varignon, 1719. Draft. Answer to 63, printed Maccl. Corres. Vol. II. p. 436.

65. James Stirling to Newton, Aug. 17, 1719. Brewster, ii. 516

66. A. H. de Sallengre to Newton, Sept. 22, 1719.

67. Joh. Bernouilli to Newton, Dec. 21, 1719. Brewster, ii. 504.

68. „ „ Newton, III. Non. Quintil. [July 5] 1719. Brewster, ii. 502.

69. Joh. Bernouilli to Newton. Copy of latter part of do. in Newton's hand.

70. Varignon to Newton, after April 28, 1720.

71. „ „ „ Nov. 28, 1720. Brewster, ii. 496.

72. James Wilson to Newton, Dec. 15, 1720 (signed A. B.). Brewster, ii. 440.

73. Rizzetti to the Royal Society, containing objections to Newton's Optical Experiments (s. d.).

Also a letter of Rizzetti to Christino Martinello, of Venice, on the same subject.

74. James Wilson to Newton, Jan. 21, 1720—1. Brewster, ii. 443.

75. Cotet to Newton, on the edition of Newton's Opticks printing at Paris, Aug. 16, 1721.

76. G. J. Gravesande to Newton, Aug. 18, 1721.

77. Varignon to Newton, Sept. 18, 1721.

78. „ „ „ Oct. 2, 1721.

79. Letter from Hen. Fr. Daguesseau to Newton, Oct. 1721.

80. Varignon to Newton, Dec. 9, 1721.

81, 82. Varignon to Bernouilli, 2 copies, April 4, 1722.

83. Varignon to Newton, April 4, 1722.

84. „ „ „ April 28, 1722.

85. „ „ „ Aug. 4, 1722.

86. Newton to Varignon. Draft reply to 83.

87. „ „ „ July (?) 13, 1722.

88, 89. Newton to Varignon. Draft. About August, 1722. 2 copies.

90. Fontenelle to Newton, Nov. 22, 1722.

91. Draft of a letter from Newton to Fontenelle. No date.

92. Newton to Varignon, Dec. 13, 1722. Draft.

93. Letter from Newton to some one at Paris about Varignon's picture after Varignon's death, which took place Dec. 23, 1722. Brewster, p. 295.

94. Joh. Bernouilli to Newton, Feb. 6, 1723. Brewster, ii. 507.

95. Philip Naudé to Newton, on the Calculus, Feb. 6, 1723–4.

96. De L'Isle to Newton, thanking him for his election to the Royal Society, April 2, 1724.

97. G. Cavelier to Newton, on the publication of his Chronology, May 11, 1724.

98. A. F. Marsili to Newton, Aug. 1724.

99. De L'Isle to Newton, Dec. 21, 1724.

100. A. F. Marsili to Newton, March 11, 1724—5.

101. G. Cavelier to Newton, March 20, 1724—5, about publication of his Chronology.

102. J. T. Desaguliers to Newton, April 29, 1725.

103. Jombert to Newton, Sept. 12, 1725. (2 copies.)

104. Draft of a letter from Newton to Daguesseau on Bernouilli's letter, complaining of being called 'eques errationis.'

105. Colin Maclaurin to Newton, Oct. 25, 1725. Brewster, ii. 385.

106. Fontenelle to Newton, acknowledging the receipt of the third edition of the Principia, July 14, 1726.

107. Thomas Mason to Conduitt, March 23, 1726–7.

108. J. Craig to Conduitt, April 7, 1727, partly printed by Brewster, ii. 315.

109. William Stukeley to Dr Mead, June 26, 1727—July 15, 1727, four sheets, written consecutively, but sent at intervals.

110. W. Stukeley to Conduitt, July 15, 1727.

111. 　　　　„　　　„　　　„　　　July 22, 1727.

* XV.

LIST OF THE LETTERS OF NEWTON, MOSTLY PUB-
LISHED IN THE MACCLESFIELD CORREPSONDENCE.

These are fair copies.

					No.
Newton to Collins	Jan.	1669	Maccl. Corr.		ccxxiv
,,	,, .	Feb. 6, 1669	,,	,,	ccxxv
,,	——	Feb. 23, 1668–9	,,	,,	ccxxvi
and comment by Collins					
Newton to Aston		May 18, 1669	,,	,,	ccxxvii
,,	Collins	Feb. 18, 1669–70	,,	,,	ccxxviii
	..	July 11, 1670	,,	,,	ccxxix
		July 16, 1670	,,	,,	ccxxxi
	,,	Sept. 27, 1670	,,	,,	ccxxxiii
	,,	July 20, 1671	,,	,,	ccxxxiv
,,	Oldenburg	Jan. 6, 1671–2	,,	,,	ccxxxv
	..	Jan. 18, 1671–2	,,	,,	ccxxxvi
		Jau. 29, 1671–2	,,	,,	ccxxxvii
		Feb. 10, 1671–2	,,	,,	ccxxxviii
		Feb. 20, 1671–2	,,	,,	ccxxxix
		March 26, 1672	Phil. Trans.		No. 82, p. 4032
		March 30, 1672	,,	,,	No. 82, p. 4034
		April 13, 1672	,,	,,	No. 83, p. 4059
	..	May 4, 1672	,,	,,	No. 83, p. 4057
	,,	May 21, 1672	not in Phil. Trans.		
,,	Collins	May 25, 1672	Maccl. Corr.		ccxli
,,	Oldenburg	June 19, 1672	,,	,,	ccxlii
	,,	July 6, 1672	,,	,,	ccxliii
	,,	July 11, 1672	Phil. Trans.		No. 88, p. 5084
,,	a long letter on Optics in reply to Mr Hook's "Considerations".				
,,	Collins	July 13, 1672	Maccl. Corr.		ccxlv
,,	Oldenburg	July 13, 1672	,,	,,	ccxlvi
,,	Collins	July 30, 1672	,,	,,	ccxlvii
,,	Oldenburg	Sept. 21, 1672	,,	,,	ccxlix
	,,	March 8, 1673	,,	,,	ccli
,,	Oldenburg?	April 3, 1673	,, .	,,	cclii
,,	in answer to Hugenius' letter of Jan. 14, 1673.				
Newton to Collins		April 9, 1673	,,	,,	ccliii
,,	,,	May 20, 1673	,,	,,	ccliv

Newton to	Collins	Sept. 17, 1673	Maccl. Corr. CCLV
,,	,,	Nov. 17, 1674	,, ,, CCLVIII
,,	Oldenburg	Dec. 9, 1674	,, ,, CCLIX
		[printed Dec. 5 in Macc. Corr.]	
,,	Dary	Jan. 22, 1675	Maccl. Corr. CCLX
,,	Collins	July 24, 1675	,, ,, CCLXI
	,,	Aug. 27, 1675	,, ,, CCLXII
,,	Oldenburg	Dec. 14, 1675	,, ,, CCLXIII
	..	Dec. 21, 1675	,, ,, CCLXIV
		Jan. 10, 1675–6	,, ,, CCLXV
		Feb. 15, 1675–6	,, ,, CCLXVII
		Feb. 19, 1676	
		June 13, 1676.	Latin letter for Leibnitz. Comm. Epist. p. 131
,,	Collins	Sept. 5, 1676	Maccl. Corr. CCLXIX
,,	Oldenburg (?)	Oct. 24, 1676	,, ,, CCLXX
,,	Oldenburg	Nov. 18, 1676	,, ,, CCLXXIII
	..	Nov. 28, 1676	

SECTION VII.

Books.

*1.   A Theological Common-place Book, written from both ends, in Newton's hand.

2.   Four folio MS. volumes, bound in red morocco, and labelled "John Conduitt," entirely in Newton's hand.

(1)   The Chronology of Ancient Kingdoms amended. Horsley, v. pp. 28—263.

(2)   i. A short chronicle from the first memory of things in Europe to the conquest of Persia by Alexander the Great. Printed twice by Horsley, v. pp. 3—27 and pp. 267—291.

ii. Another copy of the Chronology of Ancient Kingdoms amended.

(3)   Observations on the Prophecies. Horsley, v. pp. 297—491.

(4)   De motu Corporum Liber Secundus.

This is the treatise De Mundi Systemate. Horsley, iii. pp. 180—242.

*3.   A volume of extracts on Alchemical subjects, in Newton's hand.

4.   (1) A copy of the 1st edition of the Principia, interleaved with notes in Newton's hand. Among the leaves inserted is the preface to the 3rd edition. In a miserable plight from damp and ill-treatment.

(2)   A copy of the second edition of the Principia, interleaved with notes and additions in Newton's hand.

5.   A MS. copy of a portion of the Arithmetica Universalis, apparently an early copy.

6.   A copy of Schooten's edition of Des Cartes' Geometry, Lugd. 1649, with a few notes in Newton's hand.

7.   A short treatise on the beginning of Algebra, in Newton's hand: at the other end are extracts from Quintus Curtius, and a long prayer, and a sermon on Lev. xix. 18, not in N.'s hand.

8.   A common-place book written from both ends, with "Isaac Newton, Trin. Coll. Cant. 1661," in the beginning.

This contains, at one end, Definitions from Aristotle's Organon, an abridgement of the Phisiologia peripatetica of John Magirus, and some Astronomical notes by Newton: at the other, Sentences from Aristotle's Ethicks, Annotationes ex Eustachii Ethic., Axiomata,

Epitome G. J. Vossii partionum oratoriarum, a note on the word
Idea, Remarks on "Quæstiones quædam Philosophicæ," details of
the observation of the comet of 1664, of the effect of sunlight on
the eyes, etc.

*9. A copy of "Secrets revealed, or an open entrance to the shut
palace of the King," &c., by W. C., London, 1669, with notes in
Newton's hand.

*10. A bound MS. book containing at one end memoranda of
Newton's expenses at College, and at the other a short outline of
Trigonometry and Conic Sections in Newton's hand.

11, 12. Two MS. note books, bound, containing a Compendium
of Elementary Mathematics, apparently made by St John Hare.
In one of the volumes Abotesley is added to the name, and the following "Sibi, non aliis hæc." To the other volume the date 1675 is
given after the name.

13. Lettres de M. Leibnitz and M. le Chevalier Newton sur
l'invention des Fluxions et du Calcul Differentiel.

This is a proof of part of the 1st edition of Desmaizeaux's
Recueil, with corrections. (Several pages are wanting at the end.)

14. A college note-book, written from both ends, containing
early exercises—extraction of the square and cube root, elementary
Geometry, &c.—followed by annotations of Wallis's Arithmetica In-
finitorum. This is preceded by a note of Newton's fixing by an
entry in his account-book the date of the annotations as being in
the winter 1664—5, at which time he says he found the method of
infinite series. Also notes on music, chances, &c.

This is the note-book referred to in Brewster's Life of Newton,
Vol. i. p. 22.

15. Proof sheets of the edition of Newton's Opticks, with a few
MS. additions by Newton.

16. An early copy (MS.) of the Lectiones Opticæ, Jan. 1669.

17. A book, containing the commencement of a work on Hydro-
statics, the greater part consisting of a dissertation partly metaphysical, partly theistic, on the constitution of matter, motion, the
Cartesian philosophy, etc.

SECTION VIII.

MISCELLANEOUS PAPERS.

*1. Copy of the agreement relating to Sir I. Newton's MSS. Copy of bond given by Conduitt in relation to Sir I. Newton's papers. An account of John Conduitt's right to the MSS. of Sir I. Newton.

2. Six drafts (all in Newton's hand) of a scheme for establishing the Royal Society.

3. Two printed copies of Newton's letter to the Abbé Conti dated Feb. 26, 1716, with remarks of Newton on the letter of Leibnitz to the Abbé Conti—the latter dated $\frac{18}{29}$ May 1716 (printed in Des Maizeaux. Recueil, Tome ii. pp. 20, 82, 107).

4. Advertisement of the Book "De Systemate Mundi" in Conduitt's hand, with memoranda and modern letters on Newton's life.

5. On Education, &c.
On educating youth in the Universities.
Testimonial to Mr David Gregory for Astr. Prof. at Oxford.
Dr Gregory on the method of teaching in the Colleges in Scotland.
Two Chapters on Cosmography.
Beginning of "the Elements of Mechanicks."

6. Systema Mundi.

7. Miscellaneous.
An account of the System of the World described in Mr Newton's principles of Philosophy.

8. Astronomia, cap. 1, 2, 3, 4. This contains a drawing and description of a quadrant or sextant for measuring angles by reflexion.

9. Phænomena 1—15.

10. Scheme of Observations recommended to a traveller.

*11. Papers relating to legal matters.

12. General proportions for the parts of a ship.

*13. Estimates of the expenses of Government in 1668 and 1675, and a chronological tree of the royal family 1689.

N. 4

*14. John Conrad de Hatzfeld on a scheme for Perpetual Motion.

List of proposed machines by le Sieur Balesme, with fragments on finding the Longitude.

15.   Extracts from Phil. Trans. and other fragmentary Papers.

Graphical construction by Newton relating to the conjunction of Jupiter and Saturn, &c.

*16· Fragments of the Historia Cælestis.

*17. "Barometri altitudines per totum itineris mei Alpini decursum."   June 25—July 13.   No author's name or year.

*18.   Testimonial for E. Paget, M.A., *Trin., as a person fit to teach navigation to the King's satisfaction.   3 April, 1682.

19.   A scheme of Mathematical learning proposed for Mr Stone's foundation (at Christ's hospital).   Several drafts.

20.   Newton's remarks on this.

21.   Draft of his letter on the subject.

22.   Long letter by Newton in answer.

*23.   Two drafts of a paper headed, The case of Trin. Coll., on the fellowship dividends.

*24·   Henricus Sextus, apparently a College or University declamation.

*25·   A Latin phrase-book, under the heads of English words in alphabetical order, the first word *abate*, the last *conduct*.   At the other end are extracts from Epiphanius, S. Augustine, &c.

*26.   Phrases from Terence's Andria, with occasional translations.

*27.   Miscellaneous fragments relating to personal matters.   The packet contains a torn scrap of a letter from Newton's mother to him, 6 May, 1665, and one from Catharine Conduitt to Newton.

28.   A Problem in Chances, not in Newton's hand.

*29·   A Demonstration in French on the Quadrature of the Circle, by Dan Waeijwel of Amsterdam.

*30·   Scraps.

SECTION IX.

CORRESPONDENCE, ARTICLES OF AGREEMENT, &c. ABOUT THE PUBLICATION OF FLAMSTEED'S OBSERVATIONS, &c.

Catalogue of Manuscripts of Tycho Brahe.

Draft of Latin letter to Roemer relating to Tycho's observations; similar letter in English; both in Newton's handwriting.

Arbuthnot to [Newton]? July 30, 1706.

Letter from Newton and the other Referees to Prince George of Denmark concerning the publication of Flamsteed's observations, Jan. 23, 1705.

Two drafts of Articles of Agreement made between the Referees and Mr John Flamsteed.

Flamsteed to Newton, Oct. 25, 1705.

,, ,, April 10, 1708.

Copy of an Order sent to Mr Flamsteed, July 14, 1708.

Flamsteed to Sir Christopher Wren, July 19, 1708.

The Referees to Sir Isaac Newton.

Account of the expense of printing Mr John Flamsteed's Observations.

Order to pay £125 to Flamsteed for his first Catalogue of fixed stars.

Receipt for the same from Ja. Hodgson.

Flamsteed to Newton, April 23, 1716 (asking for the return of his MSS.) printed in Baily's Flamsteed. p. 322.

Order by Queen Anne for the appointment of a Board of Visitors of the Royal Observatory dated Dec. 12, 1710.

Drafts of Correspondence relating thereto.

Petition to the Queen of the President, Council and Fellows of the Royal Society of London, for the grant of a new place of Meeting.

* SECTION X.

I. CORRESPONDENCE BETWEEN CONDUITT AND FONTENELLE
ABOUT THE ÉLOGE.

Conduitt to Fontenelle,   27th March, 1727. O. S.
Fontenelle to Conduitt,   14th April, 1727. N. S.
Conduitt to Fontenelle,   No date given, but must be about 21st
                       July, 1727.
                       31st July, 1727.
     ,,   ,,   5th October, 1727. O. S.
Fontenelle to Conduitt,   15 Nov. 1727. N. S.
Conduitt to Fontenelle,   23rd Nov. 1727.
    ,,   ,,   1st Jan. 1727–8.

The above are inclosed in a portion of Mists' Weekly Journal for Saturday, April 8, 1727, containing Reflections occasioned by the Death of Sir I. Newton.

II. Conduitt's Memoirs of Sir I. Newton, sent to Fontenelle for the Éloge.

1. English copy, containing 29 numbered pages, No. 21 repeated, and 1 page of corrections.

2. French copy, containing 27 pages. This includes a translation of the account of Newton's funeral from the London Gazette of 4th April, 1727.

III. A copy of the London Gazette for 4th April, 1727, containing the account of Sir I. Newton's funeral.

DRAFTS OF FRAGMENTS OF CONDUITT'S INTENDED LIFE OF
SIR I. NEWTON.

1. 42 pages, giving an account of Newton's life to the time of his going to Cambridge.

2. 35½ pages, containing a more finished copy of the same. [This was intended to be followed by an account of the state of Philosophy when Newton began his discoveries.]

3. Four copies of suggestions addressed to some one from whom Conduitt expected to obtain a popular account of the state of philosophy when Sir I. Newton first appeared, and also a similar account of his discoveries, and of the improvements that several persons have made in various parts of them.   7½ pages.

4. 16 pages, relating to his life and work at Cambridge.

5. 17 pages of Miscellanea, containing anecdotes, &c.

6. 17 pages relating to Newton's character.

7. 2 copies, each about 1½ page, on his love and gratitude to his mother.

8. 2 pages on Sir I. Newton's manual dexterity.

9. 2 copies of 2 pages, each on the same subject, illustrated by a custom in the house of Austria.

10. Paper with date 31st of August, 1726, containing 4 large and 4 small pages, containing anecdotes of Newton, relating to various times.

11. 2 pages, containing an account of a conversation of Conduitt with Newton, on Sunday the 7th March, 1724–5.

12. 2 pages, containing various scraps from Newton's note-books.

13. Scrap of 4 small pages, on Newton's dispute with Hook.

14. Scrap of 2 small pages, in glorification of Newton.

15. Scrap of 1½ large pages, containing rough notes relating to Newton's last illness, and brief references to anecdotes.

16. A compliment on Pope.

17. Sketch of a preface.

18. Extracts from Journal books of the R. Soc. relating to the late Sir I. Newton with a letter from W. Rutty, R. S. Sec. to Conduitt.

Dates of what passed at the University (so endorsed by Conduitt).

LETTERS AND MEMORANDA, RELATING TO NEWTON, AFTER HIS DEATH.

1.   Thomas Mason to Conduitt, 13 March, 1726-7.

2.   J. Craig to Conduitt, 7 Apr. 1727, partly printed by Brewster, ii. 315.

3.   Wm. Stukeley to Conduitt, 26 June, 1727.

4.   Wm. Stukeley to Dr Mead, 26 June, 1727—15 July, 1727 (four sheets written at intervals).

5.   Dr Mead to Conduitt, 7 July, 1727.

6.   Wm. Stukeley to Conduitt, 15 July, 1727.

7.   Wm. Stukeley to Conduitt, 22 July, 1727.

8.   Memoranda of Newton, given by A. Demoivre to Conduitt, Nov. 1727 (in Conduitt's hand).

9.   Draft of a letter from Conduitt to A. Pope, 8 Nov. 1727, enclosing

10.   The dedication to the Queen of Sir I. N.'s chronology, and

11.   An account of the chief events of Newton's life.

12.   A. Pope to Conduitt, 10 Nov. 1727, printed by Brewster, ii. 521.

13.   Nicholas Wickins to Prof. Smith, 16 Jan. 1727-8, printed by Brewster, ii. 88.

14.   W. Stukeley to Conduitt, 16 Jan. 1727-8.

15.   Humphrey Newton to Conduitt, 17 Jan. 1727-8, printed by Brewster, ii. 91.

16.   J. Conduitt to ———, 6 Feb. 1727-8, printed by Brewster, i. viii.

17.   W. Stukeley to Conduitt, 13 Feb. 1727-8.

18.   Humphrey Newton to Conduitt, 14 Feb. 1727-8, printed by Brewster, ii. 95.

19.   W. Stukeley to Conduitt, 29 Feb. 1727-8.

20.   J. Conduitt to ———, 4 June, 1729 ; see Brewster i. x. n'.

21.   Bp. Sherlock to ———, 10 June, 1731.

22.   Note of Newton's elections at the Royal Society. -

23.   Nevil Maskelyne to Dr Horsley, with remarks on Horsley's ed. of Newton, by one Robison, 8 May, 1782.

*SECTION XIII.

PAPERS ON NEWTON'S FAMILY MATTERS, AND ON THE MINT.

1.   Statement of Lord Halifax's legacy to Mrs Barton, and of the transfer from the Executor George Lord Halifax, giving the date of the trust, 26 October, 1706.   With some notes on Miracles.

2.   An account of what his majesty may lose by renewing for seven years the contract with Cornwall and Devonshire for Tynn.

3.   An account of the gold and silver coined at the Mint, from 1713 to 1715, with some notes on Repentance at the back.

4.   Draft of a letter to the Lords Commissioners of the Treasury with this account, some notes on the Controversy on Fluxions at the back.

5.   The accounts of Mr Ambrose Warren, Agent for the Trustees, &c., of the charity of his Grace Thomas Archbishop of Canterbury, founded at the Tabernacle by Golden Square, for the quarter ending Christmas, 1700.

6.   Paper of calculations, apparently for the Mint.

7.   Proposal for a medal to commemorate the Union of England and Scotland.

8.   Various letters and fragments on family matters.

9.   Pedigree and papers relating to his family, all in Newton's hand excepting the pedigree, which is a copy.

---

*SECTION XIV.

BOOKS AND PAPERS NOT BY NEWTON.

1.   Essaies and Meditations concerning morality and religion. The first part.   A folio, with no author's name, written in the same hand throughout.

2.   Sir C. Wren's cipher, describing three instruments proper for discovering the longitude at sea.   In Halley's hand.   Printed by Brewster, ii. p. 263.

3. Drawing of the arms of the Swinfords of Swinford, with some notes. In Mrs Barton's hand.

4. Catherine Conduitt's will, 9 July, 1731.

5. Epitaph on F——s Ch——is (Charteris).

6. Epigrammes écrites en vieux Gaulois en imitation de Clement Marot, per Mons. Rousseau. Copied at Geneva, 1709.

7. Problem in Spherical Trigonometry, in French.

8. A scheme of the Longitude, signed Laurans.

9. Several copies (printed) of Leibnitz's Charta volans. 29 July, 1713.

10. An abridgement of a Manuscript of Sir Robert Southwell's concerning travelling. Writt. 1658, Feb. 20. Written from the other end are " Chansons Françoises."

11. A MS. of Cicero de Senectute, about 1480.

12. Treatise in French, on the Infinite Divisibility of Matter. No name ; handwriting unknown.

13. Metaphysical Speculations on Astronomy. No name ; hand unknown ; of no interest.

14. Viaticum Nautarum, or the Sailor's Vade Mecum, by Robert Wright, B.A., formerly of Jesus College in Cambridge.

15. Œdipus Sphingi, Auctore R. P. Nicolas Augustino Venetiis, 1709. (Incomplete.)

16. A MS. book on the Motions of the Secondary Planets, divided into six chapters.

17. Elementary calculations and figures relating to Spherical Trigonometry, possibly by St John Hare.

*SECTION XV.

Complimentary letters to Newton from distinguished foreigners.

UNIVERSITY PRESS, CAMBRIDGE.
August, 1888.

CATALOGUE OF

WORKS

PUBLISHED FOR THE SYNDICS

OF THE

Cambridge University Press.

London: C. J. CLAY AND SONS,
CAMBRIDGE UNIVERSITY PRESS WAREHOUSE,
AVE MARIA LANE.

GLASGOW: 263, ARGYLE STREET.

Cambridge: DEIGHTON, BELL AND CO.
Leipzig: F. A. BROCKHAUS.

750
1,8/88

The Cambridge University Press.

THE HOLY SCRIPTURES, &c.

THE CAMBRIDGE PARAGRAPH BIBLE of the Authorized English Version, with the Text Revised by a Collation of its Early and other Principal Editions, the Use of the Italic Type made uniform, the Marginal References remodelled, and a Critical Introduction prefixed, by F. H. A. SCRIVENER, M.A., LL.D., Editor of the Greek Testament, Codex Augiensis, &c., and one of the Revisers of the Authorized Version. Crown 4to. gilt. 21s.

From the Times.

"Students of the Bible should be particularly grateful (to the Cambridge University Press) for having produced, with the able assistance of Dr Scrivener, a complete critical edition of the Authorized Version of the English Bible, an edition such as, to use the words of the Editor, 'would have been executed long ago had this version been nothing more than the greatest and best known of English classics.' Falling at a time when the formal revision of this version has been undertaken by a distinguished company of scholars and divines, the publication of this edition must be considered most opportune."

From the Athenæum.

"Apart from its religious importance, the English Bible has the glory; which but few sister versions indeed can claim, of being the chief classic of the language, of having, in conjunction with Shakspeare, and in an immeasurable degree more than he, fixed the language beyond any possibility of important change. Thus the recent contributions to the literature of the subject, by such workers as Mr Francis Fry and Canon Westcott, appeal to a wide range of sympathies; and to these may now be added Dr Scrivener, well known for his labours in the cause of the Greek Testament criticism, who has brought out, for the

Syndics of the Cambridge University Press, an edition of the English Bible, according to the text of 1611, revised by a comparison with later issues on principles stated by him in his Introduction. Here he enters at length into the history of the chief editions of the version, and of such features as the marginal notes, the use of italic type, and the changes of orthography, as well as into the most interesting question as to the original texts from which our translation is produced."

From the Methodist Recorder.

"This noble quarto of over 1300 pages is in every respect worthy of editor and publishers alike. The name of the Cambridge University Press is guarantee enough for its perfection in outward form, the name of the editor is equal guarantee for the worth and accuracy of its contents. Without question, it is the best Paragraph Bible ever published, and its reduced price of a guinea brings it within reach of a large number of students."

From the London Quarterly Review.

"The work is worthy in every respect of the editor's fame, and of the Cambridge University Press. The noble English Version, to which probably never presented before in so perfect a form."

THE CAMBRIDGE PARAGRAPH BIBLE. STUDENT'S EDITION, on *good writing paper*, with one column of print and wide margin to each page for MS. notes. This edition will be found of great use to those who are engaged in the task of Biblical criticism. Two Vols. Crown 4to. gilt. 31s. 6d.

THE AUTHORIZED EDITION OF THE ENGLISH BIBLE (1611), ITS SUBSEQUENT REPRINTS AND MODERN REPRESENTATIVES. Being the Introduction to the Cambridge Paragraph Bible (1873), re-edited with corrections and additions. By F. H. A. SCRIVENER, M.A., D.C.L., LL.D., Prebendary of Exeter and Vicar of Hendon. Crown 8vo. 7s. 6d.

BREVIARIUM AD USUM INSIGNIS ECCLESIAE

SARUM. Juxta Editionem maximam pro CLAUDIO CHEVALLON ET FRANCISCO REGNAULT A.D. MDXXXI. in Alma Parisiorum Academia impressam : labore ac studio FRANCISCI PROCTER, A.M., ET CHRISTOPHORI WORDSWORTH, A.M.

FASCICULUS I. In quo continentur KALENDARIUM, et ORDO TEMPORALIS sive PROPRIUM DE TEMPORE TOTIUS ANNI, una cum ordinali suo quod usitato vocabulo dicitur PICA SIVE DIRECTORIUM SACERDOTUM. Demy 8vo. 18s.

"The value of this reprint is considerable to liturgical students, who will now be able to consult in their own libraries a work absolutely indispensable to a right understanding of the history of the Prayer-Book, but which till now usually necessitated a visit to some public library, since the rarity of the volume made its cost prohibitory to all but a few. .... Messrs Procter and Wordsworth have discharged their editorial task with much care and judgment, though the conditions under which they have been working are such as to hide that fact from all but experts."—*Literary Churchman.*

FASCICULUS II. In quo continentur PSALTERIUM, cum ordinario Officii totius hebdomadae juxta Horas Canonicas, et proprio Completorii, LITANIA, COMMUNE SANCTORUM, ORDINARIUM MISSAE CUM CANONE ET XIII MISSIS, &c. &c. Demy 8vo. 12s.

"Not only experts in liturgiology, but all persons interested in the history of the Anglican Book of Common Prayer, will be grateful to the Syndicate of the Cambridge University Press for forwarding the publication of the volume which bears the above title, and which has recently appeared under their auspices."—*Notes and Queries.*

"Cambridge has worthily taken the lead with the Breviary, which is of especial value for that part of the reform of the Prayer-Book which will fit it for the wants of our time . . .

For all persons of religious tastes the Breviary, with its mixture of Psalm and Anthem and Prayer and Hymn, all hanging one on the other, and connected into a harmonious whole, must be deeply interesting."—*Church Quarterly Review.*

"The editors have done their work excellently, and deserve all praise for their labours in rendering what they justly call 'this most interesting Service-book' more readily accessible to historical and liturgica students."—*Saturday Review.*

FASCICULUS III. In quo continetur PROPRIUM SANCTORUM quod et sanctorale dicitur, una cum accentuario. Demy 8vo. 15s.

FASCICULI I. II. III. complete, £2. 2s.

BREVIARIUM ROMANUM a FRANCISCO CARDINALI

QUIGNONIO editum et recognitum iuxta editionem Venetiis A.D. 1535 impressam curante JOHANNE WICKHAM LEGG Societatis Antiquariorum atque Collegii Regalis Medicorum Londinensium Socio in Nosocomio Sancti Bartholomaei olim Praelectore. Demy 8vo. 12s.

GREEK AND ENGLISH TESTAMENT, in parallel

Columns on the same page. Edited by J. SCHOLEFIELD, M.A. Small Octavo. New Edition, with the Marginal References as arranged and revised by Dr SCRIVENER. Cloth, red edges. 7s. 6d.

GREEK AND ENGLISH TESTAMENT. THE STU-

DENT'S EDITION of the above, on *large writing paper.* 4to. 12s.

GREEK TESTAMENT, ex editione Stephani tertia, 1550.

Small 8vo. 3s. 6d.

THE NEW TESTAMENT IN GREEK according to the

text followed in the Authorised Version, with the Variations adopted in the Revised Version. Edited by F. H. A. SCRIVENER, M.A., D.C.L., LL.D. Crown 8vo. 6s. Morocco boards or limp. 12s. *The Revised Version is the Joint Property of the Universities of Cambridge and Oxford.*

THE PARALLEL NEW TESTAMENT GREEK AND

ENGLISH, being the Authorised Version set forth in 1611 Arranged in Parallel Columns with the Revised Version of 1881, and with the original Greek, as edited by F. H. A. SCRIVENER, M.A., D.C.L., LL.D. Crown 8vo. 12s. 6d. *The Revised Version is the Joint Property of the Universities of Cambridge and Oxford.*

London: C. J. CLAY & SONS, Cambridge University Press Warehouse,
Ave Maria Lane.

THE OLD TESTAMENT IN GREEK ACCORDING TO THE SEPTUAGINT.

Edited by H. B. SWETE, D.D., Honorary Fellow of Gonville and Caius College. Vol. I. Genesis— IV Kings. Crown 8vo. 7s. 6d.

Volume II. By the same Editor.   [*In the Press.*

"The Edition has been executed in the very best style of Cambridge accuracy, which has no superior anywhere, and this is enough to put it at the head of the list of editions for manual use."—*Academy.*

THE BOOK OF ECCLESIASTES, with Notes and Introduction.

By the Very Rev. E. H. PLUMPTRE, D.D., Dean of Wells. Large Paper Edition. Demy 8vo. 7s. 6d.

"No one can say that the Old Testament is a dull or worn-out subject after reading this singularly attractive and also instructive commentary. Its wealth of literary and historical illustration surpasses anything to which we can point in English exegesis of the Old Testament; indeed, even Delitzsch, whose pride it is to leave no source of illustration unexplored, is far inferior on this head to Dr Plumptre."—*Academy*, Sept. 10, 1881.

THE GOSPEL ACCORDING TO ST MATTHEW

in Anglo-Saxon and Northumbrian Versions, synoptically arranged: with Collations exhibiting all the Readings of all the MSS. Edited by the Rev. W. W. SKEAT, Litt.D., Elrington and Bosworth Professor of Anglo-Saxon. **New Edition.** Demy 4to. 10s.

THE GOSPEL ACCORDING TO ST MARK, uniform

with the preceding, by the same Editor. Demy 4to. 10s.

THE GOSPEL ACCORDING TO ST LUKE, uniform

with the preceding, by the same Editor. Demy 4to. 10s.

THE GOSPEL ACCORDING TO ST JOHN, uniform

with the preceding, by the same Editor. Demy 4to. 10s.

"*The Gospel according to St John, in Anglo-Saxon and Northumbrian Versions:* Edited for the Syndics of the University Press, by the Rev. Walter W. Skeat, M.A., completes an undertaking designed and commenced by that distinguished scholar, J. M. Kemble, some forty years ago. Of the particular volume now before us, we can only say it is worthy of its two predecessors. We repeat that the service rendered to the study of Anglo-Saxon by this Synoptic collection cannot easily be overstated."—*Contemporary Review.*

THE POINTED PRAYER BOOK, being the Book of

Common Prayer with the Psalter or Psalms of David, pointed as they are to be sung or said in Churches. Royal 24mo. 1s. 6d.

The same in square 32mo. cloth. 6d.

THE CAMBRIDGE PSALTER, for the use of Choirs and

Organists. Specially adapted for Congregations in which the "Cambridge Pointed Prayer Book" is used. Demy 8vo. cloth extra, 3s. 6d. cloth limp, cut flush. 2s. 6d.

THE PARAGRAPH PSALTER, arranged for the use of

Choirs by BROOKE FOSS WESTCOTT, D.D., Regius Professor of Divinity in the University of Cambridge. Fcap. 4to. 5s.

The same in royal 32mo. Cloth 1s. Leather 1s. 6d.

"The Paragraph Psalter exhibits all the care, thought, and learning that those acquainted with the works of the Regius Professor of Divinity at Cambridge would expect to find, and there is not a clergyman or organist in England who should be without this Psalter as a work of reference."—*Morning Post.*

THE MISSING FRAGMENT OF THE LATIN TRANS-LATION OF THE FOURTH BOOK OF EZRA,

discovered, and edited with an Introduction and Notes, and a facsimile of the MS., by ROBERT L. BENSLY, M.A., Lord Almoner's Professor of Arabic. Demy 4to. 10s.

"It has been said of this book that it has added a new chapter to the Bible, and, startling as the statement may at first sight appear, it is no exaggeration of the actual fact, if by the Bible we understand that of the larger size which contains the Apocrypha, and if the Second Book of Esdras can be fairly called a part of the Apocrypha."—*Saturday Review.*

THE ORIGIN OF THE LEICESTER CODEX OF THE NEW TESTAMENT.

By J. RENDEL HARRIS, M.A. With 3 plates. Demy 4to. 10s. 6d.

London: C. J. CLAY & SONS, Cambridge University Press Warehouse, Ave Maria Lane.

CODEX S. CEADDAE LATINUS. Evangelia SSS.
Matthaei, Marci, Lucae ad cap. III. 9 complectens, circa septinum vel octavum saeculum scriptvs, in Ecclesia Cathedrali Lichfieldiensi servatus. Cum codice versionis Vulgatae Amiatino contulit, prolegomena conscripsit, F. H. A. SCRIVENER, A.M., D.C.L., LL.D., With 3 plates. £1. 1s.

THEOLOGY—(ANCIENT).

THE GREEK LITURGIES. Chiefly from original Authorities. By C. A. SWAINSON, D.D., late Master of Christ's College, Cambridge. Crown 4to. Paper covers. 15s.

"Jeder folgende Forscher wird dankbar anerkennen, dass Swainson das Fundament zu einer historisch-kritischen Geschichte der Griechischen Liturgien sicher gelegt hat."— ADOLPH HARNACK, *Theologische Literatur-Zeitung.*

THEODORE OF MOPSUESTIA'S COMMENTARY ON THE MINOR EPISTLES OF S. PAUL. The Latin Version with the Greek Fragments, edited from the MSS. with Notes and an Introduction, by H. B. SWETE, D.D. In Two Volumes. Volume I., containing the Introduction, with Facsimiles of the MSS., and the Commentary upon Galatians—Colossians. Demy 8vo. 12s.

"In dem oben verzeichneten Buche liegt uns die erste Hälfte einer vollständigen, ebenso sorgfältig gearbeiteten wie schön ausgestatteten Ausgabe des Commentars mit ausführlichen Prolegomena und reichhaltigen kritischen und erläuternden Anmerkungen vor."— *Literarisches Centralblatt.*

"It is the result of thorough, careful, and patient investigation of all the points bearing on the subject, and the results are presented with admirable good sense and modesty."— *Guardian.*

"Auf Grund dieser Quellen ist der Text bei Swete mit musterhafter Akribie hergestellt. Aber auch sonst hat der Herausgeber mit unermüdlichem Fleisse und eingehendster Sachkenntniss sein Werk mit allen denjenigen Zugaben ausgerüstet, welche bei einer solchen Text-Ausgabe nur irgend erwartet werden können. . . . Von den drei Haupt-

handschriften . . . sind vortreffliche photographische Facsimile's beigegeben, wie überhaupt das ganze Werk von der *University Press* zu Cambridge mit bekannter Eleganz ausgestattet ist."—*Theologische Literaturzeitung.*

"It is a hopeful sign, amid forebodings which arise about the theological learning of the Universities, that we have before us the first instalment of a thoroughly scientific and painstaking work, commenced at Cambridge and completed at a country rectory."— *Church Quarterly Review* (Jan. 1881).

"Hernn Swete's Leistung ist eine so tüchtige dass wir das Werk in keinen besseren Händen wissen möchten, und mit den sichersten Erwartungen auf das Gelingen der Fortsetzung entgegen sehen."—*Göttingische gelehrte Anzeigen* (Sept. 1881).

VOLUME II., containing the Commentary on 1 Thessalonians—Philemon, Appendices and Indices. 12s.

"Eine Ausgabe . . . für welche alle zugänglichen Hülfsmittel in musterhafter Weise benützt wurden . . . eine reife Frucht siebenjährigen Fleisses."—*Theologische Literaturzeitung* (Sept. 23, 1882).

"Mit derselben Sorgfalt bearbeitet die wir bei dem ersten Theile gerühmt haben."— *Literarisches Centralblatt* (July 29, 1882).

"M. Jacobi...commença...une édition du texte. Ce travail a été repris en Angleterre et

mené à bien, dans les deux volumes que je signale en ce moment...Elle est accompagnée de notes érudites, suivie de divers appendices, parmi lesquels on appréciera surtout un recueil des fragments des oeuvres dogmatiques de Théodore, et précédée d'une introduction où sont traitées à fond toutes les questions d'histoire littéraire qui se rattachent soit au commentaire lui-même, soit à sa version Latine."— *Bulletin Critique*, 1885.

SAYINGS OF THE JEWISH FATHERS, comprising Pirqe Aboth and Pereq R. Meir in Hebrew and English, with Critical and Illustrative Notes. By CHARLES TAYLOR, D.D., Master of St John's College, Cambridge. Demy 8vo. 10s.

"The 'Masseketh Aboth' stands at the head of Hebrew non-canonical writings. It is of ancient date, claiming to contain the dicta of teachers who flourished from B.C. 200 to the same year of our era. Mr Taylor's explanatory and illustrative commentary is very full and satisfactory."—*Spectator.*

"A careful and thorough edition which does credit to English scholarship, of a short treatise from the Mishna, containing a series of sentences or maxims ascribed mostly to Jewish teachers immediately preceding, or immediately following the Christian era. . . ."—*Contemporary Review.*

London: C. J. CLAY & SONS, Cambridge University Press Warehouse, Ave Maria Lane.

A COLLATION OF THE ATHOS CODEX OF THE
SHEPHERD OF HERMAS. Together with an Introduction by
SPYR. P. LAMBROS, PH. D., translated and edited with a Preface and
Appendices by J. ARMITAGE ROBINSON, M.A., Fellow and Dean of
Christ's College, Cambridge. Demy 8vo. 3s. 6d.

THE PALESTINIAN MISHNA. By W. H. LOWE, M.A.,
Lecturer in Hebrew at Christ's College, Cambridge. Royal 8vo. 21s.

SANCTI IRENÆI EPISCOPI LUGDUNENSIS libros
quinque adversus Hæreses, versione Latina cum Codicibus Claro-
montano ac Arundeliano denuo collata, præmissa de placitis Gnos-
ticorum prolusione, fragmenta necnon Græce, Syriace, Armeniace,
commentatione perpetua et indicibus variis edidit W. WIGAN
HARVEY, S.T.B. Collegii Regalis olim Socius. 2 Vols. 8vo. 18s.

M. MINUCII FELICIS OCTAVIUS. The text revised
from the original MS., with an English Commentary, Analysis, Introduction, and Copious Indices. Edited by H. A. HOLDEN, LL.D.
Examiner in Greek to the University of London. Crown 8vo. 7s. 6d.

THEOPHILI EPISCOPI ANTIOCHENSIS LIBRI
TRES AD AUTOLYCUM edidit, Prolegomenis Versione Notulis
Indicibus instruxit G. G. HUMPHRY, S.T.B. Post 8vo. 5s.

THEOPHYLACTI IN EVANGELIUM S. MATTHÆI
COMMENTARIUS, edited by W. G. HUMPHRY, B.D. Prebendary
of St Paul's, late Fellow of Trinity College. Demy 8vo. 7s. 6d.

TERTULLIANUS DE CORONA MILITIS, DE SPEC-
TACULIS, DE IDOLOLATRIA, with Analysis and English Notes,
by GEORGE CURREY, D.D. Preacher at the Charter House, late
Fellow and Tutor of St John's College. Crown 8vo. 5s.

FRAGMENTS OF PHILO AND JOSEPHUS. Newly
edited by J. RENDEL HARRIS, M.A., Fellow of Clare College,
Cambridge. With two Facsimiles. Demy 4to. 12s. 6d.

THE TEACHING OF THE APOSTLES. Newly edited,
with Facsimile Text and Commentary, by J. RENDEL HARRIS, M.A.
Demy 4to. £1. 1s.

THEOLOGY—(ENGLISH).

WORKS OF ISAAC BARROW, compared with the Ori-
ginal MSS., enlarged with Materials hitherto unpublished. A new
Edition, by A. NAPIER, M.A. 9 Vols. Demy 8vo. £3. 3s.

TREATISE OF THE POPE'S SUPREMACY, and a
Discourse concerning the Unity of the Church, by ISAAC BARROW.
Demy 8vo. 7s. 6d.

PEARSON'S EXPOSITION OF THE CREED, edited
by TEMPLE CHEVALLIER, B.D. New Edition. Revised by R. SINKER,
B.D., Librarian of Trinity College. Demy 8vo. 12s.

"A new edition of Bishop Pearson's famous work *On the Creed* has just been issued by the Cambridge University Press. It is the well-known edition of Temple Chevallier, thoroughly overhauled by the Rev. R. Sinker, of Trinity College. The whole text and notes have been most carefully examined and corrected, and special pains have been taken to verify the almost innumerable references. These have been more clearly and accurately given in very many places, and the citations themselves have been adapted to the best and newest texts of the several authors—texts which have undergone vast improvements within the last two centuries. The Indices have also been revised and enlarged......Altogether this appears to be the most complete and convenient edition as yet published of a work which has long been recognised in all quarters as a standard one."—*Guardian.*

AN ANALYSIS OF THE EXPOSITION OF THE

CREED written by the Right Rev. JOHN PEARSON, D.D. late Lord Bishop of Chester, by W. H. MILL, D.D. Demy 8vo. 5s.

WHEATLY ON THE COMMON PRAYER, edited by

G. E. CORRIE, D.D. late Master of Jesus College. Demy 8vo. 7s. 6d.

TWO FORMS OF PRAYER OF THE TIME OF QUEEN

ELIZABETH. Now First Reprinted. Demy 8vo. 6d.

"From 'Collections and Notes' 1867—1876, by W. Carew Hazlitt (p. 340), we learn that— 'A very remarkable volume, in the original vellum cover, and containing 25 Forms of Prayer of the reign of Elizabeth, each with the autograph of Humphrey Dyson, has lately fallen into the hands of my friend Mr H. Pyne. It is mentioned specially in the Preface to the Par-ker Society's volume of Occasional Forms of Prayer, but it had been lost sight of for 200 years.' By the kindness of the present possessor of this valuable volume, containing in all 25 distinct publications, I am enabled to re-print in the following pages the two Forms of Prayer supposed to have been lost."—*Extract from the* PREFACE.

CÆSAR MORGAN'S INVESTIGATION OF THE

TRINITY OF PLATO, and of Philo Judæus, and of the effects which an attachment to their writings had upon the principles and reasonings of the Fathers of the Christian Church. Revised by H. A. HOLDEN, LL.D. Crown 8vo. 4s.

SELECT DISCOURSES, by JOHN SMITH, late Fellow of

Queens' College, Cambridge. Edited by H. G. WILLIAMS, B.D. late Professor of Arabic. Royal 8vo. 7s. 6d.

"The 'Select Discourses' of John Smith, collected and published from his papers after his death, are, in my opinion, much the most considerable work left to us by this Cambridge School [the Cambridge Platonists]. They have a right to a place in English literary history." —Mr MATTHEW ARNOLD, in the *Contemporary Review*.

"Of all the products of the Cambridge School, the 'Select Discourses' are perhaps the highest, as they are the most accessible and the most widely appreciated...and indeed no spiritually thoughtful mind can read them unmoved. They carry us so directly into an atmosphere of divine philosophy, luminous with the richest lights of meditative genius... He was one of those rare thinkers in whom largeness of view, and depth, and wealth of poetic and speculative insight, only served to evoke more fully the religious spirit, and while he drew the mould of his thought from Plotinus, he vivified the substance of it from St Paul."—Principal TULLOCH, *Rational Theology in England in the 17th Century*.

"We may instance Mr Henry Griffin Williams's revised edition of Mr John Smith's 'Select Discourses,' which have won Mr Matthew Arnold's admiration, as an example of worthy work for an University Press to undertake."—*Times*.

THE HOMILIES, with Various Readings, and the Quo-

tations from the Fathers given at length in the Original Languages. Edited by the late G. E. CORRIE, D.D. Demy 8vo. 7s. 6d.

DE OBLIGATIONE CONSCIENTIÆ PRÆLECTIONES

decem Oxonii in Schola Theologica habitæ a ROBERTO SANDERSON, SS. Theologiæ ibidem Professore Regio. With English Notes, including an abridged Translation, by W. WHEWELL, D.D. late Master of Trinity College. Demy 8vo. 7s. 6d.

ARCHBISHOP USHER'S ANSWER TO A JESUIT,

with other Tracts on Popery. Edited by J. SCHOLEFIELD, M.A. late Regius Professor of Greek in the University. Demy 8vo. 7s. 6d.

WILSON'S ILLUSTRATION OF THE METHOD OF

explaining the New Testament, by the early opinions of Jews and Christians concerning Christ. Edited by T. TURTON, D.D. 8vo. 5s.

LECTURES ON DIVINITY delivered in the University

of Cambridge, by JOHN HEY, D.D. Third Edition, revised by T. TURTON, D.D. late Lord Bishop of Ely. 2 vols. Demy 8vo. 15s.

S. AUSTIN AND HIS PLACE IN THE HISTORY

OF CHRISTIAN THOUGHT. Being the Hulsean Lectures for 1885. By W. CUNNINGHAM, B.D. Demy 8vo. Buckram, 12s. 6d.

London: C. J. CLAY & SONS, Cambridge University Press Warehouse, Ave Maria Lane.

ARABIC, SANSKRIT, SYRIAC, &c.

THE DIVYÂVADÂNA, a Collection of Early Buddhist Legends, now first edited from the Nepalese Sanskrit MSS. in Cambridge and Paris. By E. B. COWELL, M.A., Professor of Sanskrit in the University of Cambridge, and R. A. NEIL, M.A., Fellow and Lecturer of Pembroke College. Demy 8vo. 18s.

POEMS OF BEHA ED DIN ZOHEIR OF EGYPT. With a Metrical Translation, Notes and Introduction, by E. H. PALMER, M.A., Barrister-at-Law of the Middle Temple, late Lord Almoner's Professor of Arabic, formerly Fellow of St John's College, Cambridge. 2 vols. Crown 4to.

> Vol. I. The ARABIC TEXT. 10s. 6d.
> Vol. II. ENGLISH TRANSLATION. 10s. 6d.; cloth extra. 15s.

"We have no hesitation in saying that in both Prof. Palmer has made an addition to Oriental literature for which scholars should be grateful; and that, while his knowledge of Arabic is a sufficient guarantee for his mastery of the original, his English compositions are distinguished by versatility, command of language, rhythmical cadence, and, as we have remarked, by not unskilful imitations of the styles of several of our own favourite poets, living and dead."—*Saturday Review.*

"This sumptuous edition of the poems of Behá-ed-dín Zoheir is a very welcome addition to the small series of Eastern poets accessible to readers who are not Orientalists."—*Academy.*

THE CHRONICLE OF JOSHUA THE STYLITE, composed in Syriac A.D. 507 with an English translation and notes, by W. WRIGHT, LL.D., Professor of Arabic. Demy 8vo. 10s. 6d.

"Die lehrreiche kleine Chronik Josuas hat nach Assemani und Martin in Wright einen dritten Bearbeiter gefunden, der sich um die Emendation des Textes wie um die Erklärung der Realien wesentlich verdient gemacht hat ... Ws. Josua-Ausgabe ist eine sehr dankenswerte Gabe und besonders empfehlenswert als ein Lehrmittel für den syrischen Unterricht; es erscheint auch gerade zur rechten Zeit, da die zweite Ausgabe von Roedigers syrischer Chrestomathie im Buchhandel vollständig vergriffen und diejenige von Kirsch-Bernstein nur noch in wenigen Exemplaren vorhanden ist."—*Deutsche Litteraturzeitung.*

KALILAH AND DIMNAH, OR, THE FABLES OF BIDPAI; being an account of their literary history, together with an English Translation of the same, with Notes, by I. G. N. KEITH-FALCONER, M.A., late Lord Almoner's Professor of Arabic in the University of Cambridge. Demy 8vo. 7s. 6d.

NALOPÀKHYÀNAM, OR, THE TALE OF NALA; containing the Sanskrit Text in Roman Characters, followed by a Vocabulary and a sketch of Sanskrit Grammar. By the late Rev. THOMAS JARRETT, M.A. Trinity College, Regius Professor of Hebrew. Demy 8vo. 10s.

NOTES ON THE TALE OF NALA, for the use of Classical Students, by J. PEILE, Litt. D., Master of Christ's College. Demy 8vo. 12s.

CATALOGUE OF THE BUDDHIST SANSKRIT MANUSCRIPTS in the University Library, Cambridge. Edited by C. BENDALL, M.A., Fellow of Gonville and Caius College. Demy 8vo. 12s.

"It is unnecessary to state how the compilation of the present catalogue came to be placed in Mr Bendall's hands; from the character of his work it is evident the selection was judicious, and we may fairly congratulate those concerned in it on the result... Mr Bendall has entitled himself to the thanks of all Oriental scholars, and we hope he may have before him a long course of successful labour in the field he has chosen."—*Athenæum.*

HISTORY OF ALEXANDER THE SON OF PHILIP THE KING OF THE MACEDONIANS. Syriac Text and English Translation, by E. A. BUDGE, B.A., Christ's College.

GREEK AND LATIN CLASSICS, &c.

SOPHOCLES: The Plays and Fragments, with Critical Notes, Commentary, and Translation in English Prose,. by R. C. JEBB, Litt.D., LL.D., Professor of Greek in the University of Glasgow.
Part I. Oedipus Tyrannus. Demy 8vo. *New Edition.* 12*s.* 6*d.*
Part II. Oedipus Coloneus. Demy 8vo. 12*s.* 6*d.*
Part III. Antigone. Demy 8vo. 12*s.* 6*d.*

"Of his explanatory and critical notes we can only speak with admiration. Thorough scholarship combines with taste, erudition, and boundless industry to make this first volume a pattern of editing. The work is made complete by a prose translation, upon pages alternating with the text, of which we may say shortly that it displays sound judgment and taste, without sacrificing precision to poetry of expression."—*The Times.*
"Professor Jebb's edition of Sophocles is already so fully established, and has received such appreciation in these columns and elsewhere, that we have judged this third volume when we have said that it is of a piece with the others. The whole edition so far exhibits perhaps the most complete and elaborate editorial work which has ever appeared."—*Saturday Review.*

"Prof. Jebb's keen and profound sympathy, not only with Sophocles and all the best of ancient Hellenic life and thought, but also with modern European culture, constitutes him an ideal interpreter between the ancient writer and the modern reader."—*Athenæum.*
"It would be difficult to praise this third instalment of Professor Jebb's unequalled edition of Sophocles too warmly, and it is almost a work of supererogation to praise it at all. It is equal, at least, and perhaps superior, in merit, to either of his previous instalments; and when this is said, all is said. Yet we cannot refrain from formally recognising once more the consummate Greek scholarship of the editor, and from once more doing grateful homage to his masterly tact and literary skill, and to his unwearied and marvellous industry."—*Spectator.*

AESCHYLI FABULAE.—ΙΚΕΤΙΔΕΣ ΧΟΗΦΟΡΟΙ IN LIBRO MEDICEO MENDOSE SCRIPTAE EX VV. DD. CONIECTURIS EMENDATIUS EDITAE cum Scholiis Graecis et brevi adnotatione critica, curante F. A. PALEY, M.A., LL.D. Demy 8vo. 7*s.* 6*d.*

THE AGAMEMNON OF AESCHYLUS. With a Translation in English Rhythm, and Notes Critical and Explanatory.
New Edition Revised. By BENJAMIN HALL KENNEDY, D.D., Regius Professor of Greek. Crown 8vo. 6*s.*
"One of the best editions of the masterpiece of Greek tragedy."—*Athenæum.*

THE THEÆTETUS OF PLATO with a Translation and Notes by the same Editor. Crown 8vo. 7*s.* 6*d.*

ARISTOTLE.—HEPI ΨΥΧΗΣ. ARISTOTLE'S PSYCHOLOGY, in Greek and English, with Introduction and Notes, by EDWIN WALLACE, M.A., late Fellow and Tutor of Worcester College, Oxford. Demy 8vo. 18*s.*

"The notes are exactly what such notes ought to be,—helps to the student, not mere displays of learning. By far the more valuable parts of the notes are neither critical nor literary, but philosophical and expository of the thought, and of the connection of thought, in the treatise itself. In this relation the notes are invaluable. Of the translation, it may be said that an English reader may fairly master by means of it this great treatise of Aristotle."—*Spectator.*

"Wallace's Bearbeitung der Aristotelischen Psychologie ist das Werk eines denkenden und in allen Schriften des Aristoteles und grössten-teils auch in der neueren Litteratur zu denselben belesenen Mannes... Der schwächste Teil der Arbeit ist der kritische... Aber in allen diesen Dingen liegt auch nach der Absicht des Verfassers nicht der Schwerpunkt seiner Arbeit, sondern."—Prof. Susemihl in *Philologische Wochenschrift.*

ARISTOTLE.—ΠΕΡΙ ΔΙΚΑΙΟΣΥΝΗΣ. THE FIFTH BOOK OF THE NICOMACHEAN ETHICS OF ARISTOTLE. Edited by HENRY JACKSON, Litt.D., Fellow of Trinity College, Cambridge. Demy 8vo. 6*s.*

"It is not too much to say that some of the points he discusses have never had so much light thrown upon them before.... Scholars

will hope that this is not the only portion of the Aristotelian writings which he is likely to edit."—*Athenæum.*

London: C. J. CLAY & SONS, Cambridge University Press Warehouse, Ave Maria Lane.

ARISTOTLE. THE RHETORIC. With a Commentary

by the late E. M. COPE, Fellow of Trinity College, Cambridge, revised and edited by J. E. SANDYS, Litt.D. With a biographical Memoir by the late H. A. J. MUNRO, Litt.D. 3 Vols., Demy 8vo. **Now reduced to 21s.** (*originally published at 31s. 6d.*)

"This work is in many ways creditable to the University of Cambridge. If an English student wishes to have a full conception of what is contained in the *Rhetoric* of Aristotle, to Mr Cope's edition he must go."—*Academy.*

"Mr Sandys has performed his arduous duties with marked ability and admirable tact. ...... In every part of his work—revising, supplementing, and completing—he has done exceedingly well."—*Examiner.*

PINDAR. OLYMPIAN AND PYTHIAN ODES. With

Notes Explanatory and Critical, Introductions and Introductory Essays. Edited by C. A. M. FENNELL, Litt. D., late Fellow of Jesus College. Crown 8vo. 9s.

"Mr Fennell deserves the thanks of all classical students for his careful and scholarly edition of the Olympian and Pythian odes. He brings to his task the necessary enthusiasm for his author, great industry, a sound judgment, and, in particular, copious and minute learning

in comparative philology."—*Athenæum.*

"Considered simply as a contribution to the study and criticism of Pindar, Mr Fennell's edition is a work of great merit."—*Saturday Review.*

—— THE ISTHMIAN AND NEMEAN ODES. By the same Editor. Crown 8vo. 9s.

" ... As a handy and instructive edition of a difficult classic no work of recent years surpasses Mr Fennell's 'Pindar.'"—*Athenæum.*

"This work is in no way inferior to the previous volume. The commentary affords

valuable help to the study of the most difficult of Greek authors, and is enriched with notes on points of scholarship and etymology which could only have been written by a scholar of very high attainments."—*Saturday Review.*

PRIVATE ORATIONS OF DEMOSTHENES, with In-

troductions and English Notes, by F. A. PALEY, M.A. Editor of Aeschylus, etc. and J. E. SANDYS, Litt.D. Fellow and Tutor of St John's College, and Public Orator in the University of Cambridge.

PART I. Contra Phormionem, Lacritum, Pantaenetum, Boeotum de Nomine, Boeotum de Dote, Dionysodorum. **New Edition.** Crown 8vo. 6s.

"Mr Paley's scholarship is sound and accurate, his experience of editing wide, and if he is content to devote his learning and abilities to the production of such manuals as these, they will be received with gratitude throughout the higher schools of the country. Mr Sandys is deeply read in the German

literature which bears upon his author, and the elucidation of matters of daily life, in the delineation of which Demosthenes is so rich, obtains full justice at his hands. . . . We hope this edition may lead the way to a more general study of these speeches in schools than has hitherto been possible."—*Academy.*

PART II. Pro Phormione, Contra Stephanum I. II.; Nicostratum, Cononem, Calliclem. **New Edition.** Crown 8vo. 7s. 6d.

"It is long since we have come upon a work evincing more pains, scholarship, and varied research and illustration than Mr Sandys's contribution to the 'Private Orations of De-

mosthenes'."—*Saturday Review.*

" ...... the edition reflects credit on Cambridge scholarship, and ought to be extensively used."—*Athenæum.*

DEMOSTHENES AGAINST ANDROTION AND

AGAINST TIMOCRATES, with Introductions and English Commentary, by WILLIAM WAYTE, M.A., late Professor of Greek, University College, London. Crown 8vo. 7s. 6d.

"These speeches are highly interesting, as illustrating Attic Law, as that law was influenced by the exigences of politics . . . As vigorous examples of the great orator's style, they are worthy of all admiration; and they have the advantage—not inconsiderable when the actual attainments of the average schoolboy are considered—of having an easily com-

prehended subject matter . . . . Besides a most lucid and interesting introduction, Mr Wayte has given the student effective help in his running commentary. We may note, as being so well managed as to form a very valuable part of the exegesis, the summaries given with every two or three sections throughout the speech."—*Spectator.*

PLATO'S PHÆDO, literally translated, by the late E. M.

COPE, Fellow of Trinity College, Cambridge, revised by HENRY JACKSON, Litt. D., Fellow of Trinity College. Demy 8vo. 5s.

THE BACCHAE OF EURIPIDES. With Introduction, Critical Notes, and Archæological Illustrations, by J. E. SANDYS, Litt.D. New and Enlarged Edition. Crown 8vo. 12s. 6d.

"Of the present edition of the *Bacchæ* by Mr Sandys we may safely say that never before has a Greek play, in England at least, had fuller justice done to its criticism, interpretation, and archæological illustration, whether for the young student or the more advanced scholar. The Cambridge Public Orator may be said to have taken the lead in issuing a complete edition of a Greek play, which is destined perhaps to gain redoubled favour now that the study of ancient monuments has been applied to its illustration."—*Saturday Review*.

"The volume is interspersed with well-executed woodcuts, and its general attractiveness of form reflects great credit on the University Press. In the notes Mr Sandys has more than sustained his well-earned reputation as a careful and learned editor, and shows consider-

able advance in freedom and lightness of style. . . . Under such circumstances it is superfluous to say that for the purposes of teachers and advanced students this handsome edition far surpasses all its predecessors."—*Athenæum*.

"It has not, like so many such books, been hastily produced to meet the momentary need of some particular examination; but it has employed for some years the labour and thought of a highly finished scholar, whose aim seems to have been that his book should go forth *totus teres atque rotundus*, armed at all points with all that may throw light upon its subject. The result is a work which will not only assist the schoolboy or undergraduate in his tasks, but will adorn the library of the scholar."—*The Guardian*.

THE TYPES OF GREEK COINS. By PERCY GARDNER, Litt. D., F.S.A. With 16 Autotype plates, containing photographs of Coins of all parts of the Greek World. Impl. 4to. Cloth extra, £1. 11s. 6d.; Roxburgh (Morocco back), £2. 2s.

"Professor Gardner's book is written with such lucidity and in a manner so straightforward that it may well win converts, and it may

be distinctly recommended to that omnivorous class of readers—'men in the schools'."—*Saturday Review*.

ESSAYS ON THE ART OF PHEIDIAS. By C. WALD-STEIN, Litt. D., Phil. D., Reader in Classical Archæology in the University of Cambridge. Royal 8vo. With numerous Illustrations. 16 Plates. Buckram, 30s.

"I acknowledge expressly the warm enthusiasm for ideal art which pervades the whole volume, and the sharp eye Dr Waldstein has proved himself to possess in his special line of study, namely, stylistic analysis, which has led him to several happy and important discoveries. His book will be universally welcomed as a

very valuable contribution towards a more thorough knowledge of the style of Pheidias."—*The Academy*.

"'Essays on the Art of Pheidias' form an extremely valuable and important piece of work. . . . Taking it for the illustrations alone, it is an exceedingly fascinating book."—*Times*.

AN INTRODUCTION TO GREEK EPIGRAPHY. Part I. The Archaic Inscriptions and the Greek Alphabet by E. S. ROBERTS, M.A., Fellow and Tutor of Gonville and Caius College. Demy 8vo. With illustrations. 18s.

M. TULLI CICERONIS AD. M. BRUTUM ORATOR. A revised text edited with Introductory Essays and with critical and explanatory notes, by J. E. SANDYS, Litt.D. Demy 8vo. 16s.

"This volume, which is adorned with several good woodcuts, forms a handsome and welcome addition to the Cambridge editions of Cicero's works."—*Athenæum*.

"A model edition."—*Spectator*.

"The commentary is in every way worthy of the editor's high reputation."—*Academy*.

M. TULLI CICERONIS DE FINIBUS BONORUM ET MALORUM LIBRI QUINQUE. The text revised and explained; With a Translation by JAMES S. REID, Litt. D., Fellow and Tutor of Gonville and Caius College. 3 Vols. [*In the Press.* VOL. III. Containing the Translation. Demy 8vo. 8s.

M. T. CICERONIS DE OFFICIIS LIBRI TRES, with Marginal Analysis, English Commentary, and copious Indices, by H. A. HOLDEN, LL.D. Sixth Edition, Revised and Enlarged. Cr. 8vo. 9s.

"Few editions of a classic have found so much favour as Dr Holden's *De Officiis*, and the present revision (sixth edition) makes the

position of the work secure."—*American Journal of Philology*.

M. T. CICERONIS DE OFFICIIS LIBER TERTIUS, With Introduction, Analysis and Commentary, by H. A. HOLDEN, LL.D. Crown 8vo. 2s.

London: C. J. CLAY & SONS, Cambridge University Press Warehouse, Ave Maria Lane.

M. TVLLI CICERONIS PRO C RABIRIO [PERDVELLIONIS REO] ORATIO AD QVIRITES With Notes Introduction and Appendices by W. E. HEITLAND, M.A., Fellow and Tutor of St John's College, Cambridge. Demy 8vo. 7s. 6d.

M. TULLII CICERONIS DE NATURA DEORUM Libri Tres, with Introduction and Commentary by JOSEPH B. MAYOR, M.A., together with a new collation of several of the English MSS. by J. H. SWAINSON, M.A.

Vol. I. Demy 8vo. 10s. 6d.   Vol. II. 12s. 6d.   Vol. III. 10s.

"Such editions as that of which Prof. Mayor has given us the first instalment will doubtless do much to remedy this undeserved neglect. It is one on which great pains and much learning have evidently been expended, and is in every way admirably suited to meet the needs of the student . . . The notes of the editor are all that could be expected from his well-known learning and scholarship."—*Academy.*

N. D. II. und zeigt ebenso wie der erste einen erheblichen Fortschritt gegen die bisher vorhandenen commentirten Ausgaben. Man darf jetzt, nachdem der grösste Theil erschienen ist, sagen, dass niemand, welcher sich sachlich oder kritisch mit der Schrift De Nat. Deor. beschäftigt, die neue Ausgabe wird ignoriren dürfen."—P. SCHWENCKE in *JB. f. cl. Alt.* vol. 35, p. 90 foll.

"Der vorliegende zweite Band enthält

P. VERGILI MARONIS OPERA cum Prolegomenis et Commentario Critico edidit B. H. KENNEDY, S.T.P., Graecae Linguae Prof. Regius. Extra Fcap. 8vo. 5s.

See also Pitt Press Series, pp. 24—27.

MATHEMATICS, PHYSICAL SCIENCE, &c.

MATHEMATICAL AND PHYSICAL PAPERS. By Sir W. THOMSON, LL.D., D.C.L., F.R.S., Professor of Natural Philosophy in the University of Glasgow. Collected from different Scientific Periodicals from May 1841, to the present time. Vol. I. Demy 8vo. 18s. Vol. II. 15s. [Volume III. *In the Press.*

"Wherever exact science has found a follower Sir William Thomson's name is known as a leader and a master. For a space of 40 years each of his successive contributions to knowledge in the domain of experimental and mathematical physics has been recognized as marking a stage in the progress of the subject. But, unhappily for the mere learner, he is no writer of

text-books. His eager fertility overflows into the nearest available journal . . . The papers in this volume deal largely with the subject of the dynamics of heat. They begin with two or three articles which were in part written at the age of 17, before the author had commenced residence as an undergraduate in Cambridge." —*The Times.*

MATHEMATICAL AND PHYSICAL PAPERS, by G. G. STOKES, M.A., LL.D., F.R.S., Lucasian Professor of Mathematics in the University of Cambridge. Reprinted from the Original Journals and Transactions, with Additional Notes by the Author. Vol. I. Demy 8vo. 15s. Vol. II. 15s. [Vol. III. *In the Press.*

"...The same spirit pervades the papers on pure mathematics which are included in the volume. They have a severe accuracy of style

which well befits the subtle nature of the subjects, and inspires the completest confidence in their author."—*The Times.*

A HISTORY OF THE THEORY OF ELASTICITY AND OF THE STRENGTH OF MATERIALS, from Galilei to the present time. VOL. I. Galilei to Saint-Venant, 1639-1850. By the late I. TODHUNTER, Sc.D., F.R.S., edited and completed by Professor KARL PEARSON, M.A. Demy 8vo. 25s.

Vol. II. By the same Editor.   [*In the Press.*

A TREATISE ON GEOMETRICAL OPTICS. By R. S. HEATH, M.A., Professor of Mathematics in Mason Science College, Birmingham. Demy 8vo. 12s. 6d.

AN ELEMENTARY TREATISE ON GEOMETRICAL OPTICS. By R. S. HEATH, M.A. Crown 8vo. 6s.

THE SCIENTIFIC PAPERS OF THE LATE PROF. J. CLERK MAXWELL. Edited by W. D. NIVEN, M.A. In 2 vols. Royal 4to.   [*Nearly ready.*

THE COLLECTED MATHEMATICAL PAPERS OF
ARTHUR CAYLEY, M.A., F.R.S., Sadlerian Professor of Pure
Mathematics in the University of Cambridge. Demy 4to.
[*In the Press.*

A CATALOGUE OF THE PORTSMOUTH COL-
LECTION OF BOOKS AND PAPERS written by or belonging
to SIR ISAAC NEWTON. Demy 8vo. 5s.

A TREATISE ON NATURAL PHILOSOPHY. By
Sir W. THOMSON, LL.D., D.C.L., F.R.S., and P. G. TAIT, M.A.,
Part I. Demy 8vo. 16s. **Part II.** Demy 8vo. 18s.

ELEMENTS OF NATURAL PHILOSOPHY. By Pro-
fessors Sir W. THOMSON and P. G. TAIT. Demy 8vo. 9s.

AN ATTEMPT TO TEST THE THEORIES OF
CAPILLARY ACTION by FRANCIS BASHFORTH, B.D., and
J. C. ADAMS, M.A., F.R.S. Demy 4to. £1. 1s.

A TREATISE ON THE THEORY OF DETERMI-
nants and their applications in Analysis and Geometry, by R. F.
SCOTT, M.A., Fellow of St John's College. Demy 8vo. 12s.

HYDRODYNAMICS, a Treatise on the Mathematical
Theory of the Motion of Fluids, by HORACE LAMB, M.A., formerly
Fellow of Trinity College, Cambridge. Demy 8vo. 12s.

THE ANALYTICAL THEORY OF HEAT, by JOSEPH
FOURIER. Translated, with Notes, by A. FREEMAN, M.A., formerly
Fellow of St John's College, Cambridge. Demy 8vo. 12s.

PRACTICAL WORK AT THE CAVENDISH LABORA-
TORY. HEAT. Edited by W. N. SHAW, M.A. Demy 8vo. 3s.

THE ELECTRICAL RESEARCHES OF THE Hon. H.
CAVENDISH, F.R.S. Written between 1771 and 1781. Edited from
the original MSS. in the possession of the Duke of Devonshire, K. G.,
by the late J. CLERK MAXWELL, F.R.S. Demy 8vo. 18s.

AN ELEMENTARY TREATISE ON QUATERNIONS.
By P. G. TAIT, M.A. *Second Edition.* Demy 8vo. 14s.

THE MATHEMATICAL WORKS OF ISAAC BAR-
ROW, D.D. Edited by W. WHEWELL, D.D. Demy 8vo. 7s. 6d.

COUNTERPOINT. A Practical Course of Study, by the
late Professor Sir G. A. MACFARREN, M.A., Mus. Doc. New
Edition, revised. Crown 4to. 7s. 6d.

A TREATISE ON THE GENERAL PRINCIPLES OF
CHEMISTRY, by M. M. PATTISON MUIR, M.A., Fellow and Præ-
lector in Chemistry of Gonville and Caius College. Demy 8vo. 15s.
[*New Edition. In the Press.*

"The value of the book as a digest of the historical developments of chemical thought is immense."—*Academy.*

"Theoretical Chemistry has moved so rapidly of late years that most of our ordinary text books have been left far behind. German students, to be sure, possess an excellent guide to the present state of the science in 'Die Modernen Theorien der Chemie' of Prof. Lothar Meyer; but in this country the student has had to content himself with such works as Dr Tilden's 'Introduction to Chemical Philosophy', an admirable book in its way, but rather slender. Mr Pattison Muir having aimed at a more comprehensive scheme, has produced a systematic treatise on the principles of chemical philosophy which stands far in advance of any kindred work in our language. It is a treatise that requires for its due comprehension a fair acquaintance with physical science, and it can hardly be placed with advantage in the hands of any one who does not possess an extended knowledge of descriptive chemistry. But the advanced student whose mind is well equipped with an array of chemical and physical facts can turn to Mr Muir's masterly volume for unfailing help in acquiring a knowledge of the principles of modern chemistry."—*Athenæum.*

ELEMENTARY CHEMISTRY. By M. M. PATTISON
MUIR, M.A., and CHARLES SLATER, M.A., M.B. Crown 8vo. 4s. 6d.

PRACTICAL CHEMISTRY. A Course of Laboratory
Work. By M. M. PATTISON MUIR, M.A., and D. J. CARNEGIE, B.A.
Crown 8vo. 3s.

NOTES ON QUALITATIVE ANALYSIS. Concise and Explanatory. By H. J. H. FENTON, M.A., F.I.C., Demonstrator of Chemistry in the University of Cambridge. Cr. 4to. *New Edition.* 6s.

LECTURES ON THE PHYSIOLOGY OF PLANTS, by S. H. VINES, D.Sc., Fellow of Christ's College. Demy 8vo. With Illustrations. 21s.

"To say that Dr Vines' book is a most valuable addition to our own botanical literature is but a narrow meed of praise: it is a work which will take its place as cosmopolitan: no more clear or concise discussion of the difficult chemistry of metabolism has appeared.... In erudition it stands alone among English books, and will compare favourably with any foreign competitors."—*Nature.*
"It has long been a reproach to English

science that the works in most general use in this country for higher botanical teaching have been of foreign origin. ...This is not as it should be; and we welcome Dr Vines' Lectures on the Physiology of Plants as an important step towards the removal of this reproach....The work forms an important contribution to the literature of the subject....It will be eagerly welcomed by all students, and must be in the hands of all teachers."—*Academy.*

A SHORT HISTORY OF GREEK MATHEMATICS. By J. GOW, Litt.D., Fellow of Trinity College. Demy 8vo. 10s. 6d.

DIOPHANTOS OF ALEXANDRIA; a Study in the History of Greek Algebra. By T. L. HEATH, M.A., Fellow of Trinity College, Cambridge. Demy 8vo. 7s. 6d.

"This study in the history of Greek Algebra is an exceedingly valuable contribution to the history of mathematics."—*Academy.*
"The most thorough account extant of Diophantus's place, work, and critics. . . . [The

classification of Diophantus's methods of solution taken in conjunction with the invaluable abstract, presents the English reader with a capital picture of what Greek algebraists had really accomplished.]"—*Athenæum.*

THE FOSSILS AND PALÆONTOLOGICAL AFFINITIES OF THE NEOCOMIAN DEPOSITS OF UPWARE AND BRICKHILL with Plates, being the Sedgwick Prize Essay for the Year 1879. By the late W. KEEPING, M.A., F.G.S. Demy 8vo. 10s. 6d.

A CATALOGUE OF BOOKS AND PAPERS ON PROTOZOA, CŒLENTERATES, WORMS, and certain smaller groups of animals, published during the years 1861—1883, by D'ARCY W. THOMPSON, M.A. Demy 8vo. 12s. 6d.

ASTRONOMICAL OBSERVATIONS made at the Observatory of Cambridge by the late Rév. JAMES CHALLIS, M.A., F.R.S., F.R.A.S. For various Years, from 1846 to 1860.

ASTRONOMICAL OBSERVATIONS from 1861 to 1865. Vol. XXI. Royal 4to. 15s. From 1866 to 1869. Vol. XXII. Royal 4to. [*Nearly ready.*

A CATALOGUE OF THE COLLECTION OF BIRDS formed by the late H. E. STRICKLAND, now in the possession of the University of Cambridge. By O. SALVIN, M.A. Demy 8vo. £1. 1s.

A CATALOGUE OF AUSTRALIAN FOSSILS, Stratigraphically and Zoologically arranged, by R. ETHERIDGE, Jun., F.G.S. Demy 8vo. 10s. 6d.

ILLUSTRATIONS OF COMPARATIVE ANATOMY, VERTEBRATE AND INVERTEBRATE, for the Use of Students in the Museum of Zoology and Comparative Anatomy. Second Edition. Demy 8vo. 2s. 6d.

A CATALOGUE OF THE COLLECTION OF CAMBRIAN AND SILURIAN FOSSILS contained in the Geological Museum of the University of Cambridge, by J. W. SALTER, F.G.S. With a Portrait of PROFESSOR SEDGWICK. Royal 4to. 7s. 6d.

CATALOGUE OF OSTEOLOGICAL SPECIMENS contained in the Anatomical Museum of the University of Cambridge. Demy 8vo. 2s. 6d.

London: C. J. CLAY & SONS, Cambridge University Press Warehouse, Ave Maria Lane.

LAW.

A SELECTION OF CASES ON THE ENGLISH LAW
OF CONTRACT. By GERARD BROWN FINCH, M.A., of Lincoln's Inn, Barrister at Law; Law Lecturer and late Fellow of Queens' College, Cambridge. Royal 8vo. 28s.

"An invaluable guide towards the best method of legal study."—*Law Quarterly Review.*

THE INFLUENCE OF THE ROMAN LAW ON
THE LAW OF ENGLAND. Being the Yorke Prize Essay for 1884. By T. E. SCRUTTON, M.A. Demy 8vo. 10s. 6d.

"Legal work of just the kind that a learned University should promote by its prizes."—*Law Quarterly Review.*

LAND IN FETTERS. Being the Yorke Prize Essay for
1885. By T. E. SCRUTTON, M.A. Demy 8vo. 7s. 6d.

COMMONS AND COMMON FIELDS, OR THE HIS-
TORY AND POLICY OF THE LAWS RELATING TO COMMONS AND ENCLOSURES IN ENGLAND. Being the Yorke Prize Essay for 1886. By T. E. SCRUTTON, M.A. Demy 8vo. 10s. 6d.

HISTORY OF THE LAW OF TITHES IN ENGLAND.
Being the Yorke Prize Essay for 1887. By W. EASTERBY, B.A., LL.B. St John's College and the Middle Temple. Demy 8vo. 7s. 6d.

AN ANALYSIS OF CRIMINAL LIABILITY. By E. C.
CLARK, LL.D., Regius Professor of Civil Law in the University of Cambridge, also of Lincoln's Inn, Barrister-at-Law. Crown 8vo. 7s. 6d.

PRACTICAL JURISPRUDENCE, a Comment on AUSTIN.
By E. C. CLARK, LL.D. Crown 8vo. 9s.

"Damit schliesst dieses inhaltreiche und nach allen Seiten anregende Buch über Prac- tical Jurisprudence."—König. *Centralblatt für Rechtswissenschaft.*

A SELECTION OF THE STATE TRIALS. By J. W.
WILLIS-BUND, M.A., LL.B., Professor of Constitutional Law and History, University College, London. Crown 8vo. Vols. I. and II. In 3 parts. **Now reduced to 30s.** (*originally published at 46s.*)

"This work is a very useful contribution to that important branch of the constitutional history of England which is concerned with the growth and development of the law of treason, as it may be gathered from trials before the ordinary courts. The author has very wisely distinguished these cases from those of impeachment for treason before Parliament, which he proposes to treat in a future volume under the general head 'Proceedings in Parliament.'" — *The Academy.*

"This is a work of such obvious utility that the only wonder is that no one should have undertaken it before . . . In many respects therefore, although the trials are more or less abridged, this is for the ordinary student's purpose not only a more handy, but a more useful work than Howell's."—*Saturday Review.*

"But, although the book is most interesting to the historian of constitutional law, it is also not without considerable value to those who seek information with regard to procedure and the growth of the law of evidence. We should add that Mr Willis-Bund has given short prefaces and appendices to the trials, so as to form a connected narrative of the events in history to which they relate. We can thoroughly recommend the book."—*Law Times.*

"To a large class of readers Mr Willis-Bund's compilation will thus be of great assistance, for he presents in a convenient form a judicious selection of the principal statutes and the leading cases bearing on the crime of treason . . . For all classes of readers these volumes possess an indirect interest, arising from the nature of the cases themselves, from the men who were actors in them, and from the numerous points of social life which are incidentally illustrated in the course of the trials."—*Athenæum.*

THE FRAGMENTS OF THE PERPETUAL EDICT
OF SALVIUS JULIANUS, collected, arranged, and annotated by BRYAN WALKER, M.A., LL.D., late Law Lecturer of St John's College, and Fellow of Corpus Christi College, Cambridge. Crown 8vo. 6s.

"In the present book we have the fruits of the same kind of thorough and well-ordered study which was brought to bear upon the notes to the Commentaries and the Institutes . . . Hitherto the Edict has been almost inaccessible to the ordinary English student, and such a student will be interested as well as perhaps surprised to find how abundantly the extant fragments illustrate and clear up points which have attracted his attention in the Commentaries, or the Institutes, or the Digest."— *Law Times.*

London : ·C. J. CLAY & SONS, Cambridge University Press Warehouse, Ave Maria Lane.

BRACTON'S NOTE BOOK. A Collection of Cases decided in the King's Courts during the reign of Henry the Third, annotated by a Lawyer of that time, seemingly by Henry of Bratton. Edited by F. W. MAITLAND of Lincoln's Inn, Barrister at Law, Reader in English Law in the University of Cambridge. 3 vols. Demy 8vo. Buckram. £3. 3s. *Net.*

AN INTRODUCTION TO THE STUDY OF JUS-TINIAN'S DIGEST. Containing an account of its composition and of the Jurists used or referred to therein. By HENRY JOHN ROBY, M.A., formerly Prof. of Jurisprudence, University College, London. Demy 8vo. 9s.

JUSTINIAN'S DIGEST. Lib. VII., Tit. I. De Usufructu with a Legal and Philological Commentary. By H. J. ROBY, M.A. Demy 8vo. 9s.

Or the Two Parts complete in One Volume. Demy 8vo. 18s.

"Not an obscurity, philological, historical, or legal, has been left unsifted. More informing aid still has been supplied to the student of the Digest at large by a preliminary account, covering nearly 300 pages, of the mode of composition of the Digest, and of the jurists whose decisions and arguments constitute its substance. Nowhere else can a clearer view be obtained of the personal succession by which the tradition of Roman legal science was sustained and developed. Roman law, almost more than Roman legions, was the backbone of the Roman commonwealth. Mr Roby, by his careful sketch of the sages of Roman law, from Sextus Papirius, under Tarquin the Proud, to the Byzantine Bar, has contributed to render the tenacity and durability of the most enduring polity the world has ever experienced somewhat more intelligible."—*The Times.*

THE COMMENTARIES OF GAIUS AND RULES OF ULPIAN. With a Translation and Notes, by J. T. ABDY, LL.D., Judge of County Courts, late Regius Professor of Laws in the University of Cambridge, and BRYAN WALKER, M.A., LL.D., late Law Lecturer of St John's College, Cambridge, formerly Law Student of Trinity Hall and Chancellor's Medallist for Legal Studies. New Edition by BRYAN WALKER. Crown 8vo. 16s.

"As scholars and as editors Messrs Abdy and Walker have done their work well ... For one thing the editors deserve special commendation. They have presented Gaius to the reader with few notes and those merely by way of reference or necessary explanation. Thus the Roman jurist is allowed to speak for himself, and the reader feels that he is really studying Roman law in the original, and not a fanciful representation of it."—*Athenæum.*

THE INSTITUTES OF JUSTINIAN, translated with Notes by J. T. ABDY, LL.D., and the late BRYAN WALKER, M.A., LL.D. Crown 8vo. 16s.

"We welcome here a valuable contribution to the study of jurisprudence. The text of the *Institutes* is occasionally perplexing, even to practised scholars, whose knowledge of classical models does not always avail them in dealing with the technicalities of legal phraseology. Nor can the ordinary dictionaries be expected to furnish all the help that is wanted. This translation will then be of great use. To the ordinary student, whose attention is distracted from the subject-matter by the difficulty of struggling through the language in which it is contained, it will be almost indispensable."—*Spectator.*

"The notes are learned and carefully compiled, and this edition will be found useful to students."—*Law Times.*

SELECTED TITLES FROM THE DIGEST, annotated by the late B. WALKER, M.A., LL.D. Part I. Mandati vel Contra. Digest XVII. 1. Crown 8vo. 5s.

—— Part II. De Adquirendo rerum dominio and De Adquirenda vel amittenda possessione. Digest XLI. 1 and 11. Crown 8vo. 6s.

—— Part III. De Condictionibus. Digest XII. 1 and 4—7 and Digest XIII. 1—3. Crown 8vo. 6s.

GROTIUS DE JURE BELLI ET PACIS, with the Notes of Barbeyrac and others; accompanied by an abridged Translation of the Text, by W. WHEWELL, D.D. late Master of Trinity College. 3 Vols. Demy 8vo. 12s. The translation separate, 6s.

HISTORY.

LIFE AND TIMES OF STEIN, OR GERMANY AND PRUSSIA IN THE NAPOLEONIC AGE, by J. R. SEELEY, M.A., Regius Professor of Modern History in the University of Cambridge, with Portraits and Maps. 3 Vols. Demy 8vo. 30s.

" DR BUSCH's volume has made people think and talk even more than usual of Prince Bismarck, and Professor Seeley's very learned work on Stein will turn attention to an earlier and an almost equally eminent German statesman. It has been the good fortune of Prince Bismarck to help to raise Prussia to a position which she had never before attained, and to complete the work of German unification. The frustrated labours of Stein in the same field were also very great, and well worthy to be taken into account. He was one, perhaps the chief, of the illustrious group of strangers who came to the rescue of Prussia in her darkest hour, about the time of the inglorious Peace of Tilsit, and who laboured to put life and order into her dispirited army, her impoverished finances, and her inefficient Civil Service. Stein strove, too, —no man more,—for the cause of unification when it seemed almost folly to hope for success. Englishmen will feel very pardonable pride at seeing one of their countrymen undertake to write the history of a period from the investigation of which even laborious Germans are apt to shrink."—*Times.*

"In a notice of this kind scant justice can be done to a work like the one before us; no short *résumé* can give even the most meagre notion of the contents of these volumes, which contain no page that is superfluous, and none that is uninteresting . . . . To understand the Germany of to-day one must study the Germany of many yesterdays, and now that study has been made easy by this work, to which no one can hesitate to assign a very high place among those recent histories which have aimed at original research."—*Athenæum.*

"We congratulate Cambridge and her Professor of History on the appearance of such a noteworthy production. And we may add that it is something upon which we may congratulate England that on the especial field of the Germans, history, on the history of their own country, by the use of their own literary weapons, an Englishman has produced a history of Germany in the Napoleonic age far superior to any that exists in German."—*Examiner.*

THE DESPATCHES OF EARL GOWER, English Ambassador at the court of Versailles from June 1790 to August 1792, to which are added the Despatches of Mr Lindsay and Mr Munro, and the Diary of Lord Palmerston in France during July and August 1791. Edited by OSCAR BROWNING, M.A., Fellow of King's College, Cambridge. Demy 8vo. 15s.

THE GROWTH OF ENGLISH INDUSTRY AND COMMERCE. By W. CUNNINGHAM, B.D., late Deputy to the Knightbridge Professor in the University of Cambridge. With Maps and Charts. Crown 8vo. 12s.

"Mr Cunningham is not likely to disappoint any readers except such as begin by mistaking the character of his book. He does not promise, and does not give, an account of the dimensions to which English industry and commerce have grown. It is with the process of growth that he is concerned; and this process he traces with the philosophical insight which distinguishes between what is important and what is trivial."—*Guardian.*

CHRONOLOGICAL TABLES OF GREEK HISTORY. Accompanied by a short narrative of events, with references to the sources of information and extracts from the ancient authorities, by CARL PETER. Translated from the German by G. CHAWNER, M.A., Fellow of King's College, Cambridge. Demy 4to. 10s.

KINSHIP AND MARRIAGE IN EARLY ARABIA, by W. ROBERTSON SMITH, M.A., LL.D., Fellow of Christ's College and University Librarian. Crown 8vo. 7s. 6d.

"It would be superfluous to praise a book so learned and masterly as Professor Robertson Smith's; it is enough to say that no student of early history can afford to be without *Kinship in Early Arabia.*"—*Nature.*

"It is clearly and vividly written, full of curious and picturesque material, and incident-ally throws light, not merely on the social history of Arabia, but on the earlier passages of Old Testament history . . . . We must be grateful to him for so valuable a contribution to the early history of social organisation."—*Scotsman.*

*London: C. J. CLAY & SONS, Cambridge University Press Warehouse,
Ave Maria Lane.*

TRAVELS IN NORTHERN ARABIA IN 1876 AND
1877. By CHARLES M. DOUGHTY, of Gonville and Caius College. With Illustrations and a Map. 2 vols. Demy 8vo. £3. 3s.

"This is in several respects a remarkable book. It records the ten years' travels of the author throughout Northern Arabia, in the Hejas and Nejd, from Syria to Mecca. No doubt this region has been visited by previous travellers, but none, we venture to think, have done their work with so much thoroughness or with more enthusiasm and love."—*Times.*

"We judge this book to be the most remarkable record of adventure and research which has been published to this generation."—*Spectator.*
"Its value as a storehouse of knowledge simply cannot be exaggerated."—*Saturday Review.*

HISTORY OF NEPAL, translated by MUNSHĪ SHEW
SHUNKER SINGH and PANDIT SHRĪ GUNĀNAND; edited with an Introductory Sketch of the Country and People by Dr D. WRIGHT, late Residency Surgeon at Kāthmāndū, and with facsimiles of native drawings, and portraits of Sir JUNG BAHĀDUR, the KING OF NEPĀL, &c. Super-royal 8vo. 10s. 6d.

"The Cambridge University Press have done well in publishing this work. Such translations are valuable not only to the historian but also to the ethnologist; ... Dr Wright's

Introduction is based on personal inquiry and observation, is written intelligently and candidly, and adds much to the value of the volume"—*Nature.*

A JOURNEY OF LITERARY AND ARCHÆOLOGICAL
RESEARCH IN NEPAL AND NORTHERN INDIA, during the Winter of 1884-5. By CECIL BENDALL, M.A., Fellow of Gonville and Caius College, Cambridge; Professor of Sanskrit in University College, London. Demy 8vo. 10s.

THE UNIVERSITY OF CAMBRIDGE FROM THE
EARLIEST TIMES TO THE ROYAL INJUNCTIONS OF 1535, by J. B. MULLINGER, M.A., Lecturer on History and Librarian to St John's College. Part I. Demy 8vo. (734 pp.), 12s.
Part II. From the Royal Injunctions of 1535 to the Accession of Charles the First. Demy 8vo. 18s.

"That Mr Mullinger's work should admit of being regarded as a continuous narrative, in which character it has no predecessors worth mentioning, is one of the many advantages it possesses over annalistic compilations, even so valuable as Cooper's, as well as over *Athenae.*"—Prof. A. W. Ward in the *Academy.*
"Mr Mullinger's narrative omits nothing which is required by the fullest interpretation of his subject. He shews in the statutes of the Colleges, the internal organization of the University, its connection with national problems, its studies, its social life, and the

activity of its leading members. All this he combines in a form which is eminently readable."— PROF. CREIGHTON in *Cont. Review.*
"Mr Mullinger has succeeded perfectly in presenting the earnest and thoughtful student with a thorough and trustworthy history."—*Guardian.*
"Mr Mullinger displays an admirable thoroughness in his work. Nothing could be more exhaustive and conscientious than his method: and his style...is picturesque and elevated."—*Times.*

HISTORY OF THE COLLEGE OF ST JOHN THE
EVANGELIST, by THOMAS BAKER, B.D., Ejected Fellow. Edited by JOHN E. B. MAYOR, M.A. Two Vols. Demy 8vo. 24s.

"To antiquaries the book will be a source of almost inexhaustible amusement, by historians it will be found a work of considerable service on questions respecting our social progress in past times; and the care and thoroughness with which Mr Mayor has discharged his editorial functions are creditable to his learning and industry."—*Athenæum.*

"The work displays very wide reading, and it will be of great use to members of the college and of the university, and, perhaps, of still greater use to students of English history, ecclesiastical, political, social, literary and academical, who have hitherto had to be content with 'Dyer.'"—*Academy.*

SCHOLAE ACADEMICAE: some Account of the Studies
at the English Universities in the Eighteenth Century. By CHRISTOPHER WORDSWORTH, M.A., Fellow of Peterhouse. Demy 8vo. 10s. 6d.

"Mr Wordsworth has collected a great quantity of minute and curious information about the working of Cambridge institutions in the last century, with an occasional comparison of the corresponding state of things at Oxford. ... To a great extent it is purely a book of reference, and as such it will be of permanent value for the historical knowledge of English

education and learning."—*Saturday Review.*
"Of the whole volume it may be said that it is a genuine service rendered to the study of University history, and that the habits of thought of any writer educated at either seat of learning in the last century will, in many cases, be far better understood after a consideration of the materials here collected."—*Academy.*

London: C. J. CLAY & SONS, Cambridge University Press Warehouse, Ave Maria Lane.

THE ARCHITECTURAL HISTORY OF THE UNI-
VERSITY OF CAMBRIDGE AND OF THE COLLEGES OF
CAMBRIDGE AND ETON, by the late ROBERT WILLIS, M.A.
F.R.S., Jacksonian Professor in the University of Cambridge. Edited
with large Additions and brought up to the present time by JOHN
WILLIS CLARK, M.A., formerly Fellow of Trinity College, Cam-
bridge. Four Vols. Super Royal 8vo. £6. 6s.

Also a limited. Edition of the same, consisting of 120 numbered
Copies only, large paper Quarto; the woodcuts and steel engravings
mounted on India paper; price Twenty-five Guineas **net** each set.

MISCELLANEOUS.

A LATIN-ENGLISH DICTIONARY. Printed from the
(Incomplete) MS. of the late T. H. KEY, M.A., F.R.S. Crown 4to.
£1. 11s. 6d.

A CATALOGUE OF ANCIENT MARBLES IN GREAT
BRITAIN, by Prof. ADOLF MICHAELIS. Translated by C. A. M.
FENNELL, Litt. D., late Fellow of Jesus College. Royal 8vo. Rox-
burgh (Morocco back), £2. 2s.

"The object of the present work of Michaelis is to describe and make known the vast
treasures of ancient sculpture now accumulated
in the galleries of Great Britain. ... Waagen gave
to the private collections of pictures the advantage of his inspection and cultivated acquaintance with art, and now Michaelis per-
forms the same office for the still less known
private hoards of antique sculptures for which
our country is so remarkable. The book is
beautifully executed, and with its few handsome
plates, and excellent indexes, does much credit
to the Cambridge Press. It has not been printed
in German, but appears for the first time in the
English translation. All lovers of true art and
of good work should be grateful to the Syndics
of the University Press for the liberal facilities
afforded by them towards the production of
this important volume by Professor Michaelis."
—*Saturday Review.*

"Professor Michaelis has achieved so high
a fame as an authority in classical archæology
that it seems unnecessary to say how good
a book this is."—*The Antiquary.*

RHODES IN ANCIENT TIMES. By CECIL TORR, M.A.
With six plates. Demy 8vo. 10s. 6d.

RHODES IN MODERN TIMES. By the same Author.
With three plates. Demy 8vo. 8s.

CHAPTERS ON ENGLISH METRE. By Rev. JOSEPH
B. MAYOR, M.A. Demy 8vo. 7s. 6d.

THE WOODCUTTERS OF THE NETHERLANDS
during the last quarter of the Fifteenth Century. In three parts.
I. History of the Woodcutters. II. Catalogue of their Woodcuts.
III. List of the Books containing Woodcuts. By WILLIAM MARTIN
CONWAY. Demy 8vo. 10s. 6d.

THE LITERATURE OF THE FRENCH RENAIS-
SANCE. An Introductory Essay. By A. A. TILLEY, M.A., Fellow
and Tutor of King's College, Cambridge. Crown 8vo. 6s.

A GRAMMAR OF THE IRISH LANGUAGE. By Prof.
WINDISCH. Translated by Dr NORMAN MOORE. Crown 8vo. 7s. 6d.

LECTURES ON TEACHING, delivered in the University
of Cambridge in the Lent Term, 1880. By J. G. FITCH, M.A., LL.D.
Her Majesty's Inspector of Training Colleges. Cr. 8vo. New Edit. 5s.

"As principal of a training college and as a
Government inspector of schools, Mr Fitch has
got at his fingers' ends the working of primary
education, while as assistant commissioner to
the late Endowed Schools Commission he has
seen something of the machinery of our higher
schools ... Mr Fitch's book covers so wide a
field and touches on so many burning questions
that we must be content to recommend it as
the best existing *vade mecum* for the teacher."
—*Pall Mall Gazette.*

For other books on Education, see Pitt Press Series, pp. 30, 31.

*London: C. J. CLAY & SONS, Cambridge University Press Warehouse,
Ave Maria Lane.*

EPISTVLAE ORTELIANAE. ABRAHAMI ORTELII (Geographi Antverpiensis) et virorvm ervditorvm ad evndem et ad JACOBVM COLIVM ORTELIANVM (Abrahami Ortelii sororis filivm) Epistvlae. Cvm aliqvot aliis epistvlis et tractatibvs qvibvsdam ab vtroqve collectis (1524—1628). Ex avtographis mandante Ecclesia Londino-batava edidit JOANNES HENRICVS HESSELS. Demy 4to. £3. 10s. *Net.*

FROM SHAKESPEARE TO POPE: an Inquiry into the causes and phenomena of the rise of Classical Poetry in England. By EDMUND GOSSE, M.A. Crown 8vo. 6s.

STUDIES IN THE LITERARY RELATIONS OF ENGLAND WITH GERMANY IN THE SIXTEENTH CENTURY. By C. H. HERFORD, M.A. Crown 8vo. 9s.

ADMISSIONS TO GONVILLE AND CAIUS COLLEGE IN THE UNIVERSITY OF CAMBRIDGE March 1558—9 to Jan. 1678—9. Edited by J. VENN, Sc.D., Senior Fellow of the College, and S. C. VENN. Demy 8vo. 10s.

CATALOGUE OF THE HEBREW MANUSCRIPTS preserved in the University Library, Cambridge. By Dr S. M. SCHILLER-SZINESSY. Volume I. containing Section I. *The Holy Scriptures;* Section II. *Commentaries on the Bible.* Demy 8vo. 9s.

A CATALOGUE OF THE MANUSCRIPTS preserved in the Library of the University of Cambridge. Demy 8vo. 5 Vols. 10s. each. INDEX TO THE CATALOGUE. Demy 8vo. 10s.

A CATALOGUE OF ADVERSARIA and printed books containing MS. notes, preserved in the Library of the University of Cambridge. 3s. 6d.

THE ILLUMINATED MANUSCRIPTS IN THE LI- brary of the Fitzwilliam Museum, Catalogued with Descriptions, and an Introduction, by W. G. SEARLE, M.A. Demy 8vo. 7s. 6d.

A CHRONOLOGICAL LIST OF THE GRACES, Documents, and other Papers in the University Registry which concern the University Library. Demy 8vo. 2s. 6d.

CATALOGUS BIBLIOTHECÆ BURCKHARDTIANÆ. Demy 4to. 5s.

GRADUATI CANTABRIGIENSES: SIVE CATA- LOGUS exhibens nomina eorum quos ab Anno Academico Admissionum MDCCC usque ad octavum diem Octobris MDCCCLXXXIV gradu quocunque ornavit Academia Cantabrigiensis, e libris subscriptionum desumptus. Cura HENRICI RICHARDS LUARD S. T. P. Coll. SS. Trin. Socii atque Academiæ Registrarii. Demy 8vo. 12s. 6d.

STATUTES OF THE UNIVERSITY OF CAMBRIDGE and for the Colleges therein, made published and approved (1878—1882) under the Universities of Oxford and Cambridge Act, 1877. With an Appendix. Demy 8vo. 16s.

STATUTES OF THE UNIVERSITY OF CAMBRIDGE. With Acts of Parliament relating to the University. 8vo. 3s. 6d.

ORDINANCES OF THE UNIVERSITY OF CAM- BRIDGE. Demy 8vo., cloth. 7s. 6d.

TRUSTS, STATUTES AND DIRECTIONS affecting (1) The Professorships of the University. (2) The Scholarships and Prizes. (3) Other Gifts and Endowments. Demy 8vo. 5s.

COMPENDIUM OF UNIVERSITY REGULATIONS, for the use of persons in Statu Pupillari. Demy 8vo. 6d.

The Cambridge Bible for Schools and Colleges.

GENERAL EDITOR : THE VERY REVEREND J. J. S. PEROWNE, D.D.,
DEAN OF PETERBOROUGH.

"It is difficult to commend too highly this excellent series."—*Guardian.*

"The modesty of the general title of this series has, we believe, led many to misunderstand its character and underrate its value. The books are well suited for study in the upper forms of our best schools, but not the less are they adapted to the wants of all Bible students who are not specialists. We doubt, indeed, whether any of the numerous popular commentaries recently issued in this country will be found more serviceable for general use."—*Academy.*

"One of the most popular and useful literary enterprises of the nineteenth century."—*Baptist Magazine.*

"Of great value. The whole series of comments for schools is highly esteemed by students capable of forming a judgment. The books are scholarly without being pretentious: information is so given as to be easily understood."—*Sword and Trowel.*

The Very Reverend J. J. S. PEROWNE, D.D., Dean of Peterborough, has undertaken the general editorial supervision of the work, assisted by a staff of eminent coadjutors. Some of the books have been already edited or undertaken by the following gentlemen :

Rev. A. CARR, M.A., *late Assistant Master at Wellington College.*

Rev. T. K. CHEYNE, M.A., D.D., *late Fellow of Balliol College, Oxford.*

Rev. S. COX, *Nottingham.*

Rev. A. B. DAVIDSON, D.D., *Professor of Hebrew, Edinburgh.*

The Ven. F. W. FARRAR, D.D., *Archdeacon of Westminster.*

Rev. C. D. GINSBURG, LL.D.

Rev. A. E. HUMPHREYS, M.A., *late Fellow of Trinity College, Cambridge.*

Rev. A. F. KIRKPATRICK, M.A., *Fellow of Trinity College, Regius Professor of Hebrew.*

Rev. J. J. LIAS, M.A., *late Professor at St David's College, Lampeter.*

Rev. J. R. LUMBY, D.D., *Norrisian Professor of Divinity.*

Rev. G. F. MACLEAR, D.D., *Warden of St Augustine's College, Canterbury.*

Rev. H. C. G. MOULE, M.A., *late Fellow of Trinity College, Principal of Ridley Hall, Cambridge.*

Rev. W. F. MOULTON, D.D., *Head Master of the Leys School, Cambridge.*

Rev. E. H. PEROWNE, D.D., *Master of Corpus Christi College, Cambridge.*

The Ven. T. T. PEROWNE, B.D., *Archdeacon of Norwich.*

Rev. A. PLUMMER, M.A., D.D., *Master of University College, Durham.*

The Very Rev. E. H. PLUMPTRE, D.D., *Dean of Wells.*

Rev. H. E. RYLE, M.A., *Hulsean Professor of Divinity.*

Rev. W. SIMCOX, M.A., *Rector of Weyhill, Hants.*

W. ROBERTSON SMITH, M.A., *Fellow of Christ's College, and University Librarian.*

The Very Rev. H. D. M. SPENCE, M.A., *Dean of Gloucester.*

Rev. A. W. STREANE, M.A., *Fellow of Corpus Christi College, Cambridge.*

London: C. J. CLAY & SONS, *Cambridge University Press Warehouse,* *Ave Maria Lane.*

THE CAMBRIDGE BIBLE FOR SCHOOLS & COLLEGES.
Continued.
Now Ready.   Cloth, Extra Fcap. 8vo.

THE BOOK OF JOSHUA.   By the Rev. G. F. MACLEAR, D.D. With 2 Maps.   2s. 6d.

THE BOOK OF JUDGES.   By the Rev. J. J. LIAS, M.A. With Map.   3s. 6d.

THE FIRST BOOK OF SAMUEL.   By the Rev. Professor KIRKPATRICK, M.A.   With Map.   3s. 6d.

THE SECOND BOOK OF SAMUEL.   By the Rev. Professor KIRKPATRICK, M.A.   With 2 Maps.   3s. 6d.

THE FIRST BOOK OF KINGS. By Rev. Prof. LUMBY, D.D.   3s. 6d.

THE SECOND BOOK OF KINGS.   By the same Editor.   3s. 6d.

THE BOOK OF JOB.   By the Rev. A. B. DAVIDSON, D.D.   5s.

THE BOOK OF ECCLESIASTES.   By the Very Rev. E. H. PLUMPTRE, D.D., Dean of Wells.   5s.

THE BOOK OF JEREMIAH.   By the Rev. A. W. STREANE, M.A.   With Map.   4s. 6d.

THE BOOK OF HOSEA.   By Rev. T. K. CHEYNE, M.A., D.D.   3s.

THE BOOKS OF OBADIAH AND JONAH.   By Archdeacon PEROWNE.   2s. 6d.

THE BOOK OF MICAH.   By Rev. T. K. CHEYNE, D.D.   1s. 6d.

THE BOOKS OF HAGGAI AND ZECHARIAH.   By Archdeacon PEROWNE.   3s.

THE GOSPEL ACCORDING TO ST MATTHEW.   By the Rev. A. CARR, M.A.   With 2 Maps.   2s. 6d.

THE GOSPEL ACCORDING TO ST MARK.   By the Rev. G. F. MACLEAR, D.D.   With 4 Maps.   2s. 6d.

THE GOSPEL ACCORDING TO ST LUKE.   By Archdeacon F. W. FARRAR.   With 4 Maps.   4s. 6d.

THE GOSPEL ACCORDING TO ST JOHN.   By the Rev. A. PLUMMER, M.A., D.D.   With 4 Maps.   4s. 6d.

THE ACTS OF THE APOSTLES.   By the Rev. Professor LUMBY, D.D.   With 4 Maps.   4s. 6d.

THE EPISTLE TO THE ROMANS.   By the Rev. H. C. G. MOULE, M.A.   3s. 6d.

THE FIRST EPISTLE TO THE CORINTHIANS.   By the Rev. J. J. LIAS, M.A.   With a Map and Plan.   2s.

THE SECOND EPISTLE TO THE CORINTHIANS.   By the Rev. J. J. LIAS, M.A.   2s.

THE EPISTLE TO THE EPHESIANS.   By the Rev. H. C. G. MOULE, M.A.   2s. 6d.

THE EPISTLE TO THE HEBREWS.   By Arch. FARRAR.   3s. 6d.

THE GENERAL EPISTLE OF ST JAMES.   By the Very Rev. E. H. PLUMPTRE, D.D., Dean of Wells.   1s. 6d.

THE EPISTLES OF ST PETER AND ST JUDE.   By the same Editor.   2s. 6d.

THE CAMBRIDGE BIBLE FOR SCHOOLS & COLLEGES.
Continued.
Preparing.

THE BOOK OF GENESIS. By the Very Rev. the DEAN OF PETERBOROUGH.

THE BOOKS OF EXODUS, NUMBERS AND DEUTERO-NOMY. By the Rev. C. D. GINSBURG, LL.D.

THE BOOKS OF EZRA AND NEHEMIAH. By the Rev. Prof. RYLE, M.A.

THE BOOK OF PSALMS. By the Rev. Prof. KIRKPATRICK, M.A.

THE BOOK OF ISAIAH. By W. ROBERTSON SMITH, M.A.

THE BOOK OF EZEKIEL. By the Rev. A. B. DAVIDSON, D.D.

THE EPISTLE TO THE GALATIANS. By the Rev. E. H. PEROWNE, D.D.

THE EPISTLES TO THE PHILIPPIANS, COLOSSIANS AND PHILEMON. By the Rev. H. C. G. MOULE, M.A.

THE EPISTLES TO THE THESSALONIANS. By the Rev. W. F. MOULTON, D.D.

THE BOOK OF REVELATION. By the Rev. W. SIMCOX, M.A.

THE CAMBRIDGE GREEK TESTAMENT
FOR SCHOOLS AND COLLEGES,
with a Revised Text, based on the most recent critical authorities, and English Notes, prepared under the direction of the General Editor, THE VERY REVEREND J. J. S. PEROWNE, D.D.

Now Ready.

THE GOSPEL ACCORDING TO ST MATTHEW. By the Rev. A. CARR, M.A. With 4 Maps. 4s. 6d.

"Copious illustrations, gathered from a great variety of sources, make his notes a very valuable aid to the student. They are indeed remarkably interesting, while all explanations on meanings, applications, and the like are distinguished by their lucidity and good sense."—*Pall Mall Gazette.*

THE GOSPEL ACCORDING TO ST MARK. By the Rev. G. F. MACLEAR, D.D. With 3 Maps. 4s. 6d.

"The Cambridge Greek Testament, of which Dr Maclear's edition of the Gospel according to St Mark is a volume, certainly supplies a want. Without pretending to compete with the leading commentaries, or to embody very much original research, it forms a most satisfactory introduction to the study of the New Testament in the original . . . Dr Maclear's introduction contains all that is known of St Mark's life, an account of the circumstances in which the Gospel was composed, an excellent sketch of the special characteristics of this Gospel; an analysis, and a chapter on the text of the New Testament generally . . . The work is completed by three good maps."—*Saturday Review.*

THE GOSPEL ACCORDING TO ST LUKE. By Archdeacon FARRAR. With 4 Maps. 6s.

THE GOSPEL ACCORDING TO ST JOHN. By the Rev. A. PLUMMER, M.A., D.D. With 4 Maps. 6s.

"A valuable addition has also been made to 'The Cambridge Greek Testament for Schools,' Dr Plummer's notes on 'the Gospel according to St John' are scholarly, concise, and instructive, and embody the results of much thought and wide reading."—*Expositor.*

THE ACTS OF THE APOSTLES. By the Rev. Prof. LUMBY, D.D., with 4 Maps. 6s.

THE FIRST EPISTLE TO THE CORINTHIANS. By the Rev. J. J. LIAS, M.A. 3s.

THE SECOND EPISTLE TO THE CORINTHIANS. By the Rev. J. J. LIAS, M.A. [*Preparing.*

THE EPISTLE TO THE HEBREWS. By Archdeacon FARRAR. [*In the Press.*

THE EPISTLES OF ST JOHN. By the Rev. A. PLUMMER, M.A., D.D. 4s.

London: C. J. CLAY & SONS, Cambridge University Press Warehouse, Ave Maria Lane.

THE PITT PRESS SERIES.

[Copies of the Pitt Press Series may generally be obtained bound in two parts for Class use, the text and notes in separate volumes.]

I. GREEK.

SOPHOCLES.—OEDIPUS TYRANNUS. School Edition, with Introduction and Commentary, by R. C. JEBB, Litt. D., LL.D., Professor of Greek in the University of Glasgow. 4s. 6d.

XENOPHON.—ANABASIS, BOOKS I. III. IV. and V. With a Map and English Notes by ALFRED PRETOR, M.A., Fellow of St Catharine's College, Cambridge. 2s. each.

"We welcome this addition to the other books of the *Anabasis* so ably edited by Mr Pretor. Although originally intended for the use of candidates at the university local examinations, yet this edition will be found adapted not only to meet the wants of the junior student, but even advanced scholars will find much in this work that will repay its perusal."—*The Schoolmaster.*

"Mr Pretor's 'Anabasis of Xenophon, Book IV.' displays a union of accurate Cambridge scholarship, with experience of what is required by learners gained in examining middle-class schools. The text is large and clearly printed, and the notes explain all difficulties. . . . Mr Pretor's notes seem to be all that could be wished as regards grammar, geography, and other matters."—*The Academy.*

BOOKS II. VI. and VII. By the same Editor. 2s. 6d. each.

"Another Greek text, designed it would seem for students preparing for the local examinations, is 'Xenophon's Anabasis,' Book II., with English Notes, by Alfred Pretor, M.A. The editor has exercised his usual discrimination in utilising the text and notes of Kuhner, with the occasional assistance of the best hints of Schneider, Vollbrecht and Macmichael on critical matters, and of Mr R. W. Taylor on points of history and geography. . . When Mr Pretor commits himself to Commentator's work, he is eminently helpful. . . Had we to introduce a young Greek scholar to Xenophon, we should esteem ourselves fortunate in having Pretor's text-book as our chart and guide."—*Contemporary Review.*

XENOPHON.—ANABASIS. By A. PRETOR, M.A., Text and Notes, complete in two Volumes. 7s. 6d.

XENOPHON.—AGESILAUS. The Text revised with Critical and Explanatory Notes, Introduction, Analysis, and Indices. By H. HAILSTONE, M.A., late Scholar of Peterhouse. 2s. 6d.

XENOPHON.—CYROPAEDEIA. BOOKS I. II. With Introduction, Notes and Map. By Rev. H. A. HOLDEN, M.A., LL.D. 2 vols. Vol. I. Text. Vol. II. Notes. 6s.

—— —— **BOOKS III., IV., V.** By the same Editor. 5s.

ARISTOPHANES—RANAE. With English Notes and Introduction by W. C. GREEN, M.A., late Assistant Master at Rugby School. 3s. 6d.

ARISTOPHANES—AVES. By the same Editor. *New Edition.* 3s. 6d.

"The notes to both plays are excellent. Much has been done in these two volumes to render the study of Aristophanes a real treat to a boy instead of a drudgery, by helping him to understand the fun and to express it in his mother tongue."—*The Examiner.*

ARISTOPHANES—PLUTUS. By the same Editor. 3s. 6d.

HOMER—ODYSSEY, BOOK IX. With Introduction, Notes and Appendices. By G. M. EDWARDS, M.A. 2s. 6d.

PLATONIS APOLOGIA SOCRATIS. With Introduction, Notes and Appendices by J. ADAM, M.A., Fellow and Classical Lecturer of Emmanuel College. 3s. 6d.

"A worthy representative of English Scholarship."—*Classical Review.*

—— **CRITO.** With Introduction, Notes and Appendix. By the same Editor. 2s. 6d.

"Mr Adam, already known as the author of a careful and scholarly edition of the Apology of Plato, will, we think, add to his reputation by his work upon the Crito."—*Academy.*

London: C. J. CLAY & SONS, Cambridge University Press Warehouse, Ave Maria Lane.

HERODOTUS, BOOK VIII., CHAPS. 1—90. Edited with
Notes and Introduction by E. S. SHUCKBURGH, M.A., late Fellow of
Emmanuel College. 3s. 6d.

HERODOTUS, BOOK IX., CHAPS. 1—89. By the same
Editor. 3s. 6d.

EURIPIDES. HERCULES FURENS. With Intro-
ductions, Notes and Analysis. By A. GRAY, M.A., Fellow of Jesus College,
and J. T. HUTCHINSON, M.A., Christ's College. New Edition. 2s.

EURIPIDES. HERACLEIDÆ. With Introduction and
Critical Notes by E. A. BECK, M.A., Fellow of Trinity Hall. 3s. 6d.

LUCIANI SOMNIUM CHARON PISCATOR ET DE
LUCTU, with English Notes by W. E. HEITLAND, M.A., Fellow of
St John's College, Cambridge. New Edition, with Appendix. 3s. 6d.

PLUTARCH'S LIVES OF THE GRACCHI. With Intro-
duction, Notes and Lexicon by Rev. HUBERT A. HOLDEN, M.A., LL.D. 6s.

PLUTARCH'S LIFE OF SULLA. With Introduction,
Notes, and Lexicon. By the Rev. HUBERT A. HOLDEN, M.A., LL.D. 6s.

PLUTARCH'S LIFE OF NICIAS. With Introduction
and Notes. By Rev. HUBERT A. HOLDEN, M.A., LL.D. 5s.

OUTLINES OF THE PHILOSOPHY OF ARISTOTLE.
Edited by E. WALLACE, M.A. (See p. 31.)

II. LATIN.

HORACE—EPISTLES, BOOK I. With Notes and Intro-
duction by E. S. SHUCKBURGH, M.A., late Fellow of Emmanuel College.
2s. 6d.

LIVY. BOOK XXI. With Notes, Introduction and Maps.
By M. S. DIMSDALE, M.A., Fellow of King's College. 3s. 6d.

M. T. CICERONIS DE AMICITIA. Edited by J. S.
REID, Litt. D., Fellow and Tutor of Gonville and Caius College. New
Edition, with Additions. 3s. 6d.

"Mr Reid has decidedly attained his aim, namely, 'a thorough examination of the Latinity
of the dialogue.'..... The revision of the text is most valuable, and comprehends sundry
acute corrections. . . . This volume, like Mr Reid's other editions, is a solid gain to the scholarship of the country."—*Athenæum.*

"A more distinct gain to scholarship is Mr Reid's able and thorough edition of the *De
Amicitiâ* of Cicero, a work of which, whether we regard the exhaustive introduction or the
instructive and most suggestive commentary, it would be difficult to speak too highly. . . . When
we come to the commentary, we are only amazed by its fulness in proportion to its bulk.
Nothing is overlooked which can tend to enlarge the learner's general knowledge of Ciceronian
Latin or to elucidate the text."—*Saturday Review.*

M. T. CICERONIS CATO MAJOR DE SENECTUTE.
Edited by J. S. REID, Litt. D. Revised Edition. 3s. 6d.

"The notes are excellent and scholarlike, adapted for the upper forms of public schools, and
likely to be useful even to more advanced students."—*Guardian.*

M. T. CICERONIS ORATIO PRO ARCHIA POETA.
Edited by J. S. REID, Litt. D. Revised Edition. 2s.

"It is an admirable specimen of careful editing. An Introduction tells us everything we could
wish to know about Archias, about Cicero's connexion with him, about the merits of the trial, and
the genuineness of the speech. The text is well and carefully printed. The notes are clear and
scholar-like. . . . No boy can master this little volume without feeling that he has advanced a long
step in scholarship."—*The Academy.*

M. T. CICERONIS PRO L. CORNELIO BALBO ORA-
TIO. Edited by J. S. REID, Litt. D. 1s. 6d.

"We are bound to recognize the pains devoted in the annotation of these two orations to the
minute and thorough study of their Latinity, both in the ordinary notes and in the textual
appendices."—*Saturday Review.*

London: C. J. CLAY & SONS, *Cambridge University Press Warehouse,*
Ave Maria Lane.

M. T. CICERONIS PRO. P. CORNELIO SULLA

ORATIO. Edited by J. S. REID, Litt. D. *3s. 6d.*

"Mr Reid is so well known to scholars as a commentator on Cicero that a new work from him scarcely needs any commendation of ours. His edition of the speech *Pro Sulla* is fully equal in merit to the volumes which he has already published . . . It would be difficult to speak too highly of the notes. There could be no better way of gaining an insight into the characteristics of Cicero's style and the Latinity of his period than by making a careful study of this speech with the aid of Mr Reid's commentary . . . Mr Reid's intimate knowledge of the minutest details of scholarship enables him to detect and explain the slightest points of distinction between the usages of different authors and different periods . . . The notes are followed by a valuable appendix on the text, and another on points of orthography; an excellent index brings the work to a close."—*Saturday Review.*

M. T. CICERONIS PRO CN. PLANCIO ORATIO.

Edited by H. A. HOLDEN, LL.D., Examiner in Greek to the University of London. Second Edition. *4s. 6d.*

"As a book for students this edition can have few rivals. It is enriched by an excellent introduction and a chronological table of the principal events of the life of Cicero; while in its appendix, and in the notes on the text which are added, there is much of the greatest value. The volume is neatly got up, and is in every way commendable."—*The Scotsman.*

M. T. CICERONIS IN Q. CAECILIUM DIVINATIO

ET IN C. VERREM ACTIO PRIMA. With Introduction and Notes by W. E. HEITLAND, M.A., and HERBERT COWIE, M.A., Fellows of St John's College, Cambridge. *3s.*

M. T. CICERONIS ORATIO PRO L. MURENA, with

English Introduction and Notes. By W. E. HEITLAND, M.A., Fellow and Classical Lecturer of St John's College, Cambridge. **Second Edition, carefully revised.** *3s.*

"Those students are to be deemed fortunate who have to read Cicero's lively and brilliant oration for L. Murena with Mr Heitland's handy edition, which may be pronounced 'four-square' in point of equipment, and which has, not without good reason, attained the honours of a second edition."—*Saturday Review.*

M. T. CICERONIS IN GAIUM VERREM ACTIO

PRIMA. With Introduction and Notes. By H. COWIE, M.A., Fellow of St John's College, Cambridge. *1s. 6d.*

M. T. CICERONIS ORATIO PRO T. A. MILONE,

with a Translation of Asconius' Introduction, Marginal Analysis and English Notes. Edited by the Rev. JOHN SMYTH PURTON, B.D., late President and Tutor of St Catharine's College. *2s. 6d.*

"The editorial work is excellently done."—*The Academy.*

M. T. CICERONIS SOMNIUM SCIPIONIS. With In-

troduction and Notes. By W. D. PEARMAN, M.A., Head Master of Potsdam School, Jamaica. *2s.*

M. TULLI CICERONIS ORATIO PHILIPPICA

SECUNDA. With Introduction and Notes by A. G. PESKETT, M.A., Fellow of Magdalene College. *3s. 6d.*

P. OVIDII NASONIS FASTORUM LIBER VI. With

a Plan of Rome and Notes by A. SIDGWICK, M.A., Tutor of Corpus Christi College, Oxford. *1s. 6d.*

"Mr Sidgwick's editing of the Sixth Book of Ovid's *Fasti* furnishes a careful and serviceable volume for average students. It eschews 'construes' which supersede the use of the dictionary, but gives full explanation of grammatical usages and historical and mythical allusions, besides illustrating peculiarities of style, true and false derivations, and the more remarkable variations of the text."—*Saturday Review.*

"It is eminently good and useful. . . . The Introduction is singularly clear on the astronomy of Ovid, which is properly shown to be ignorant and confused; there is an excellent little map of Rome, giving just the places mentioned in the text and no more; the notes are evidently written by a practical schoolmaster."—*The Academy.*

M. ANNAEI LUCANI PHARSALIAE LIBER

PRIMUS, edited with English Introduction and Notes by W. E. HEITLAND, M.A. and C. E. HASKINS, M.A., Fellows and Lecturers of St John's College, Cambridge. *1s. 6d.*

"A careful and scholarlike production."—*Times.*

"In nice parallels of Lucan from Latin poets and from Shakspeare, Mr Haskins and Mr Heitland deserve praise."—*Saturday Review.*

GAI IULI CAESARIS DE BELLO GALLICO COM-
MENT. I. With Maps and English Notes by A. G. Peskett, M.A., Fellow of Magdalene College, Cambridge. 1s. 6d.

In an unusually succinct introduction he gives all the preliminary and collateral information that is likely to be useful to a young student; and, wherever we have examined his notes, we have found them eminently practical and satisfying. . . . The book may well be recommended for careful study in school or college."—*Saturday Review.*

"The notes are scholarly, short, and a real help to the most elementary beginners in Latin prose."—*The Examiner.*

—— COMMENT. I. II. III. by the same Editor. 3s.

—— COMMENT. IV. AND V. AND COMMENT. VII. by the same Editor. 2s. each.

—— COMMENT. VI. AND COMMENT. VIII. by the same Editor. 1s. 6d. each.

P. VERGILI MARONIS AENEIDOS Libri I., II., III.,
IV., V., VI., VII., VIII., IX., X., XI., XII. Edited with Notes by A. Sidgwick, M.A., Tutor of Corpus Christi College, Oxford. 1s. 6d. each.

"Much more attention is given to the literary aspect of the poem than is usually paid to it in editions intended for the use of beginners. The introduction points out the distinction between primitive and literary epics, explains the purpose of the poem, and gives an outline of the story."—*Saturday Review.*

"Mr Arthur Sidgwick's 'Vergil, Aeneid, Book XII.' is worthy of his reputation, and is distinguished by the same acuteness and accuracy of knowledge, appreciation of a boy's difficulties and ingenuity and resource in meeting them, which we have on other occasions had reason to praise in these pages."—*The Academy.*

"As masterly in its clearly divided preface and appendices as in the sound and independent character of its annotations. . . . There is a great deal more in the notes than mere compilation and suggestion. . . . No difficulty is left unnoticed or unhandled."—*Saturday Review.*

—— —— BOOKS IX. X. in one volume. 3s.

—— —— BOOKS X., XI., XII. in one volume. 3s. 6d.

P. VERGILI MARONIS GEORGICON LIBRI I. II.
By the same Editor. 2s.

—— —— Libri III. IV. By the same Editor. 2s.

P. VERGILI MARONIS BUCOLICA, with Introduction
and Notes, by the same Editor. 1s. 6d.

"Few people have done so much in so small a compass, for the study of a great author."—*Academy.*

QUINTUS CURTIUS. A Portion of the History.
(Alexander in India.) By W. E. Heitland, M.A., Fellow and Lecturer of St John's College, Cambridge, and T. E. Raven, B.A., Assistant Master in Sherborne School. 3s. 6d.

"Equally commendable as a genuine addition to the existing stock of school-books is *Alexander in India*, a compilation from the eighth and ninth books of Q. Curtius, edited for the Pitt Press by Messrs Heitland and Raven. . . . The work of Curtius has merits of its own, which, in former generations, made it a favourite with English scholars, and which still make it a popular text-book in Continental schools. . . . . . The reputation of Mr Heitland is a sufficient guarantee for the scholarship of the notes, which are ample without being excessive, and the book is well furnished with all that is needful in the nature of maps, indices, and appendices."—*Academy.*

BEDA'S ECCLESIASTICAL HISTORY, BOOKS
III., IV., the Text from the very ancient MS. in the Cambridge University Library, collated with six other MSS. Edited, with a life from the German of Ebert, and with Notes, &c. by J. E. B. Mayor, M.A., Professor of Latin, and J. R. Lumby, D.D., Norrisian Professor of Divinity. Revised edition. 7s. 6d.

"To young students of English History the illustrative notes will be of great service, while the study of the texts will be a good introduction to Mediæval Latin."—*The Nonconformist.*

"In Bede's works Englishmen can go back to *origines* of their history, unequalled for form and matter by any modern European nation. Prof. Mayor has done good service in rendering a part of Bede's greatest work accessible to those who can read Latin with ease. He has adorned this edition of the third and fourth books of the 'Ecclesiastical History' with that amazing erudition for which he is unrivalled among Englishmen and rarely equalled by Germans. And however interesting and valuable the text may be, we can certainly apply to his notes the expression, *La sauce vaut mieux que le poisson.* They are literally crammed with interesting information about early English life. For though ecclesiastical in name, Bede's history treats of all parts of the national life, since the Church had points of contact with all."—*Examiner.*

BOOKS I. and II. *In the Press.*

London: C. J. Clay & Sons, Cambridge University Press Warehouse, Ave Maria Lane.

III. FRENCH.

LE PHILOSOPHE SANS LE SAVOIR. SEDAINE
Edited with Notes by Rev. H. A. BULL, M.A., late Master at Wellington
College. 2s.

RÉCITS DES TEMPS MÉROVINGIENS I—III.
THIERRY. Edited by GUSTAVE MASSON, B.A. Univ. Gallic., and A. R.
ROPES, M.A. With Map. 3s.

LA CANNE DE JONC. By A. DE VIGNY. Edited with
Notes by Rev. H. A. BULL, M.A. 2s.

BATAILLE DE DAMES. By SCRIBE and LEGOUVÉ.
Edited by Rev. H. A. BULL, M.A. 2s.

JEANNE D'ARC by A. DE LAMARTINE. With a Map
and Notes Historical and Philological and a Vocabulary by Rev. A. C.
CLAPIN, M.A., St John's College, Cambridge, and Bachelier-ès-Lettres of
the University of France. Enlarged Edition. 2s.

LE BOURGEOIS GENTILHOMME, Comédie-Ballet en
Cinq Actes. Par J.-B. POQUELIN DE MOLIÈRE (1670). With a life of
Molière and Grammatical and Philological Notes. By the same Editor. 1s.6d.

LA PICCIOLA. By X. B. SAINTINE. The Text, with
Introduction, Notes and Map, by the same Editor. 2s.

LA GUERRE. By MM. ERCKMANN-CHATRIAN. With
Map, Introduction and Commentary by the same Editor. 3s.

L'ÉCOLE DES FEMMES. MOLIÈRE. Edited with Introduction and Notes by GEORGE SAINTSBURY, M.A. 2s. 6d.

LAZARE HOCHE—PAR ÉMILE DE BONNECHOSE.
With Three Maps, Introduction and Commentary, by C. COLBECK, M.A.,
late Fellow of Trinity College, Cambridge. 2s.

LE VERRE D'EAU. A Comedy; by SCRIBE. With a
Biographical Memoir, and Grammatical, Literary and Historical Notes. By
the same Editor. 2s.
" It may be national prejudice, but we consider this edition far superior to any of the series
which hitherto have been edited exclusively by foreigners. Mr Colbeck seems better to understand the wants and difficulties of an English boy. The etymological notes especially are admirable. . . . The historical notes and introduction are a piece of thorough honest work."—*Journal
of Education.*

HISTOIRE DU SIÈCLE DE LOUIS XIV PAR
VOLTAIRE. Part I. Chaps. I.—XIII. Edited with Notes Philological and
Historical, Biographical and Geographical Indices, etc. by G. MASSON, B.A.
Univ. Gallic., and G. W. PROTHERO, M.A., Fellow of King's College, Cam-
bridge. 2s. 6d.

—— Part II. Chaps. XIV.—XXIV. With Three Maps
of the Period. By the same Editors. 2s. 6d.

—— Part III. Chap. XXV. to the end. By the same
Editors. 2s. 6d.

M. DARU, par M. C. A. SAINTE-BEUVE, (Causeries du
Lundi, Vol. IX.). With Biographical Sketch of the Author, and Notes
Philological and Historical. By GUSTAVE MASSON. 2s.

LA SUITE DU MENTEUR. A Comedy in Five Acts,
by P. CORNEILLE. Edited with Fontenelle's Memoir of the Author, Voltaire's
Critical Remarks, and Notes Philological and Historical. By GUSTAVE
MASSON. 2s.

LA JEUNE SIBÉRIENNE. LE LÉPREUX DE LA
CITÉ D'AOSTE. Tales by COUNT XAVIER DE MAISTRE. With Biographical Notice, Critical Appreciations, and Notes. By G. MASSON. 2s.

*London: C. J. CLAY & SONS, Cambridge University Press Warehouse,
Ave Maria Lane.*

LE DIRECTOIRE. (Considérations sur la Révolution Française. Troisième et quatrième parties.) .Par MADAME LA BARONNE DE STAËL-HOLSTEIN. With a Critical Notice of the Author, a Chronological Table, and Notes Historical and Philological, by G. MASSON, B.A., and G. W. PROTHERO, M.A. Revised and enlarged Edition. 2s.
"Prussia under Frederick the Great, and France under the Directory, bring us face to face respectively with periods of history which it is right should be known thoroughly, and which are well treated in the Pitt Press volumes. The latter in particular, an extract from the world-known work of Madame de Staël on the French Revolution, is beyond all praise for the excellence both of its style and of its matter."—*Times.*

DIX ANNÉES D'ÉXIL. LIVRE II. CHAPITRES 1—8. Par MADAME LA BARONNE DE STAËL-HOLSTEIN. With a Biographical Sketch of the Author, a Selection of Poetical Fragments by Madame de Staël's Contemporaries, and Notes Historical and Philological. By GUSTAVE MASSON and G. W. PROTHERO, M.A. Revised and enlarged edition. 2s.

FRÉDÉGONDE ET BRUNEHAUT. A Tragedy in Five Acts, by N. LEMERCIER. Edited with Notes, Genealogical and Chronological Tables, a Critical Introduction and a Biographical Notice. By GUSTAVE MASSON. 2s.

LE VIEUX CÉLIBATAIRE. A Comedy, by COLLIN D'HARLEVILLE. With a Biographical Memoir, and Grammatical, Literary and Historical Notes. By the same Editor. 2s.

LA MÉTROMANIE, A Comedy, by PIRON, with a Biographical Memoir, and Grammatical, Literary and Historical Notes. By the same Editor. 2s.

LASCARIS, ou LES GRECS DU XVᴱ. SIÈCLE, Nouvelle Historique, par A. F. VILLEMAIN, with a Biographical .Sketch of the Author, a Selection of Poems on Greece, and Notes Historical and Philological. By the same Editor. 2s.

LETTRES SUR L'HISTOIRE DE FRANCE (XIII— XXIV.). Par AUGUSTIN THIERRY. By GUSTAVE MASSON, B.A. and G. W. PROTHERO, M.A. With Map. 2s. 6d.

IV. GERMAN.

DOCTOR WESPE. BENEDIX. Lustspiel in fünf Aufzügen. Edited with Notes by KARL HERMANN BREUL, M.A. 3s.

SELECTED FABLES. LESSING and GELLERT. Edited with Notes by KARL HERMANN BREUL, M.A., Lecturer in German at the University of Cambridge. 3s.

DIE KARAVANE von WILHELM HAUFF. Edited with Notes by A. SCHLOTTMANN, Ph. D. 3s. 6d.

CULTURGESCHICHTLICHE NOVELLEN, von W. H. RIEHL, with Grammatical, Philological, and Historical Notes, and a Complete Index, by H. J. WOLSTENHOLME, B.A. (Lond.). 4s. 6d.

ERNST, HERZOG VON SCHWABEN. UHLAND. With Introduction and Notes. By H. J. WOLSTENHOLME, B.A. (Lond.), Lecturer in German at Newnham College, Cambridge. 3s. 6d.

ZOPF UND SCHWERT. Lustspiel in fünf Aufzügen von KARL GUTZKOW. With a Biographical and Historical Introduction, English Notes, and an Index. By the same Editor. 3s. 6d.
"We are glad to be able to notice a careful edition of K. Gutzkow's amusing comedy 'Zopf and Schwert' by Mr H. J. Wolstenholme. . . . These notes are abundant and contain references to standard grammatical works."—*Academy.*

Goethe's Knabenjahre. (1749—1759.) GOETHE'S BOYHOOD: being the First Three Books of his Autobiography. Arranged and Annotated by WILHELM WAGNER, Ph. D., late Professor at the Johanneum, Hamburg. 2s.

London: C. J. CLAY & SONS, Cambridge University Press Warehouse, Ave Maria Lane.

MENDELSSOHN'S LETTERS. Selections from. Edited
by James Sime, M.A. 3*s*.

HAUFF. DAS WIRTHSHAUS IM SPESSART. Edited
by A. Schlottmann, Ph.D., late Assistant Master at Uppingham School.
3*s*. 6*d*.

DER OBERHOF. A Tale of Westphalian Life, by Karl
Immermann. With a Life of Immermann and English Notes, by Wilhelm
Wagner, Ph.D., late Professor at the Johanneum, Hamburg. 3*s*.

A BOOK OF GERMAN DACTYLIC POETRY. Arranged and Annotated by the same Editor. 3*s*.

Der erste Kreuzzug (THE FIRST CRUSADE), by Fried-
rich von Raumer. Condensed from the Author's 'History of the Hohen-
staufen', with a life of Raumer, two Plans and English Notes. By
the same Editor. 2*s*.
"Certainly no more interesting book could be made the subject of examinations. The story
of the First Crusade has an undying interest. The notes are, on the whole, good."—*Educational
Times.*

A BOOK OF BALLADS ON GERMAN HISTORY.
Arranged and Annotated by the same Editor. 2*s*.
"It carries the reader rapidly through some of the most important incidents connected with
the German race and name, from the invasion of Italy by the Visigoths under their King Alaric,
down to the Franco-German War and the installation of the present Emperor. The notes supply
very well the connecting links between the successive periods, and exhibit in its various phases of
growth and progress, or the reverse, the vast unwieldy mass which constitutes modern Germany."
—*Times.*

DER STAAT FRIEDRICHS DES GROSSEN. By G.
Freytag. With Notes. By the same Editor. 2*s*.

GOETHE'S HERMANN AND DOROTHEA. With
an Introduction and Notes. By the same Editor. Revised edition by J. W.
Cartmell, M.A. 3*s*. 6*d*.
"The notes are among the best that we know, with the reservation that they are often too
abundant."—*Academy.*

Das Jahr 1813 (THE YEAR 1813), by F. Kohlrausch.
With English Notes. By W. Wagner. 2*s*.

V. ENGLISH.

COWLEY'S ESSAYS. With Introduction and Notes. By
the Rev. J. Rawson Lumby, D.D., Norrisian Professor of Divinity; Fellow
of St Catharine's College. 4*s*.

SIR THOMAS MORE'S UTOPIA. With Notes by the
Rev. J. Rawson Lumby, D.D. 3*s*. 6*d*.
"To Dr Lumby we must give praise unqualified and unstinted. He has done his work
admirably. . . . Every student of history, every politician, every social reformer, every one
interested in literary curiosities, every lover of English should buy and carefully read Dr
Lumby's edition of the 'Utopia.' We are afraid to say more lest we should be thought ex-
travagant, and our recommendation accordingly lose part of its force."—*The Teacher.*
"It was originally written in Latin and does not find a place on ordinary bookshelves. A very
great boon has therefore been conferred on the general English reader by the managers of the
Pitt Press Series, in the issue of a convenient little volume of *More's Utopia* not in the original
Latin, but in the quaint *English Translation thereof made by Raphe Robynson*, which adds a
linguistic interest to the intrinsic merit of the work. . . . All this has been edited in a most complete and scholarly fashion by Dr J. R. Lumby, the Norrisian Professor of Divinity, whose name
alone is a sufficient warrant for its accuracy. It is a real addition to the modern stock of classical
English literature."—*Guardian.*

BACON'S HISTORY OF THE REIGN OF KING
Henry VII. With Notes by the Rev. J. Rawson Lumby, D.D. 3*s*.

MORE'S HISTORY OF KING RICHARD III. Edited

with Notes, Glossary and Index of Names. By J. RAWSON LUMBY, D.D. to which is added the conclusion of the History of King Richard III. as given in the continuation of Hardyng's Chronicle, London, 1543. 3s. 6d.

THE TWO NOBLE KINSMEN, edited with Intro-

duction and Notes by the Rev. Professor SKEAT, Litt.D., formerly Fellow of Christ's College, Cambridge. 3s. 6d.

"This edition of a play that is well worth study, for more reasons than one, by so careful a scholar as Mr Skeat, deserves a hearty welcome."—*Athenæum.*

"Mr Skeat is a conscientious editor, and has left no difficulty unexplained."—*Times.*

LOCKE ON EDUCATION. With Introduction and Notes

by the Rev. R. H. QUICK, M.A. 3s. 6d.

"The work before us leaves nothing to be desired. It is of convenient form and reasonable price, accurately printed, and accompanied by notes which are admirable. There is no teacher too young to find this book interesting ; there is no teacher too old to find it profitable."—*The School Bulletin, New York.*

MILTON'S TRACTATE ON EDUCATION. A fac-

simile reprint from the Edition of 1673. Edited, with Introduction and Notes, by OSCAR BROWNING, M.A.

"A separate reprint of Milton's famous letter to Master Samuel Hartlib was a desideratum, and we are grateful to Mr Browning for his elegant and scholarly edition, to which is prefixed the careful *résumé* of the work given in his 'History of Educational Theories.'"—*Journal of Education.*

THEORY AND PRACTICE OF TEACHING. By the

Rev. EDWARD THRING, M.A., late Head Master of Uppingham School and Fellow of King's College, Cambridge. New Edition. 4s. 6d.

"Any attempt to summarize the contents of the volume would fail to give our readers a taste of the pleasure that its perusal has given us."—*Journal of Education.*

THE TEACHING OF MODERN LANGUAGES IN

THEORY AND PRACTICE. Two Lectures delivered in the University of Cambridge in the Lent Term, 1887. By C. COLBECK, M.A., Assistant Master of Harrow School. 2s.

GENERAL AIMS OF THE TEACHER, AND FORM

MANAGEMENT. Two Lectures delivered in the University of Cambridge in the Lent Term, 1883, by Archdeacon FARRAR, D.D., and R. B. POOLE, B.D. Head Master of Bedford Modern School. 1s. 6d.

THREE LECTURES ON THE PRACTICE OF EDU-

CATION. Delivered in the University of Cambridge in the Easter Term, 1882, under the direction of the Teachers' Training Syndicate. 2s.

JOHN AMOS COMENIUS, Bishop of the Moravians. His

Life and Educational Works, by S. S. LAURIE, A.M., F.R.S.E., Professor of the Institutes and History of Education in the University of Edinburgh. New Edition, revised. 3s. 6d.

OUTLINES OF THE PHILOSOPHY OF ARISTOTLE.

Compiled by EDWIN WALLACE, M.A., LL.D. (St Andrews), late Fellow of Worcester College, Oxford. Third Edition Enlarged. 4s. 6d.

"A judicious selection of characteristic passages, arranged in paragraphs, each of which is preceded by a masterly and perspicuous English analysis."—*Scotsman.*

"Gives in a comparatively small compass a very good sketch of Aristotle's teaching."—*Sat. Review.*

A SKETCH OF ANCIENT PHILOSOPHY FROM

THALES TO CICERO, by JOSEPH B. MAYOR, M.A. 3s. 6d.

"Professor Mayor contributes to the Pitt Press Series *A Sketch of Ancient Philosophy* in which he has endeavoured to give a general view of the philosophical systems illustrated by the genius of the masters of metaphysical and ethical science from Thales to Cicero. In the course of his sketch he takes occasion to give concise analyses of Plato's Republic, and of the Ethics and Politics of Aristotle ; and these abstracts will be to some readers not the least useful portions of the book."—*The Guardian.*

[*Other Volumes are in preparation.*]

London : C. J. CLAY & SONS, Cambridge University Press Warehouse, Ave Maria Lane.

University of Cambridge.

LOCAL EXAMINATIONS.

Examination Papers, for various years, with the *Regulations for the Examination.* Demy 8vo. 2s. each, or by Post, 2s. 2d.

Class Lists, for various years, Boys 1s., Girls 6d.

Annual Reports of the Syndicate, with Supplementary Tables showing the success and failure of the Candidates. 2s. each, by Post 2s. 3d.

HIGHER LOCAL EXAMINATIONS.

Examination Papers for various years, *to which are added the Regulations for the Examination.* Demy 8vo. 2s. each, by Post 2s. 2d.

Class Lists, for various years. 1s. By post, 1s. 2d.

Reports of the Syndicate. Demy 8vo. 1s., by Post 1s. 2d.

LOCAL LECTURES SYNDICATE.

Calendar for the years 1875—80. Fcap. 8vo. *cloth.* 2s.; for 1880—81. 1s.

TEACHERS' TRAINING SYNDICATE.

Examination Papers for various years, *to which are added the Regulations for the Examination.* Demy 8vo. 6d., by Post 7d.

CAMBRIDGE UNIVERSITY REPORTER.

Published by Authority.

Containing all the Official Notices of the University, Reports of Discussions in the Schools, and Proceedings of the Cambridge Philosophical, Antiquarian, and Philological Societies. 3d. weekly.

CAMBRIDGE UNIVERSITY EXAMINATION PAPERS.

These Papers are published in occasional numbers every Term, and in volumes for the Academical year.

VOL. XIV.	Parts 1 to 20.	PAPERS for the Year 1884—85,	15s. *cloth.*
VOL. XV.	„ 21 to 43.	„ „ 1885—86,	15s. *cloth.*
VOL. XVI.	„ 44 to 65.	„ „ 1886—87,	15s. *cloth.*

Oxford and Cambridge Schools Examinations.

Papers set in the Examination for Certificates, July, 1885. 2s. 6d.

List of Candidates who obtained Certificates at the Examination held in 1887 ; and Supplementary Tables. 6d.

Regulations of the Board for 1889. 9d.

Regulations for the Commercial Certificate, 1889. 3d.

Report of the Board for the year ending Oct. 31, 1887. 1s.

Studies from the Morphological Laboratory in the University of Cambridge.

Edited by ADAM SEDGWICK, M.A., Fellow and Lecturer of Trinity College, Cambridge. Vol. II. Part I. Royal 8vo. 10s. Vol. II. Part II. 7s. 6d. Vol. III. Part I. 7s. 6d. Vol. III. Part II. 7s. 6d.

London: C. J. CLAY AND SONS,
CAMBRIDGE UNIVERSITY PRESS WAREHOUSE,
AVE MARIA LANE.
GLASGOW: 263, ARGYLE STREET.

CAMBRIDGE: PRINTED BY C. J. CLAY, M.A. AND SONS, AT THE UNIVERSITY PRESS.

CPSIA information can be obtained
at www.ICGtesting.com
Printed in the USA
BVHW041752301118
534322BV00030B/75/P